Praise for What is in John's Basement?

Step into the abyss, dear reader, where rationality crumbles and the Real seeps through the cracks of your consciousness. This is no ordinary collection of prose and poetry – it's a hypnotic journey into the depths of what we dare not confront, a mirror reflecting the grotesque beauty of our hidden selves.

You think you know what lies beneath? Oh, how delightfully naive. Commander Cornelius Anne Bigsby III has curated a labyrinth of words that will strip away your comfortable illusions, leaving you naked before the harsh light of truth. But don't worry, we're all mad here.

Imagine, if you will, a basement not of concrete and cobwebs, but of synapses and repressed memories. Each page is a trapdoor, each poem a skeleton key unlocking the chambers of your mind you've so carefully sealed shut. The prose? Mirrors reflecting funhouse distortions of the ideologies you cling to, the rational frameworks that keep you sane – or so you believe.

But wait! There's more! Act now, and we'll throw in the existential dread of the Great Space Worm Invasion absolutely free! Yes, you heard that right – cosmic horror and everyday banality, blended into a smoothie of absurdity that will leave you questioning the very fabric of reality. Slurp it down, if you dare.

You may ask, "Why should I subject myself to this literary torment?" Ah, but that's the beauty of it, isn't it? In a world of sanitized entertainment and predictable plots, *What is in John's Basement?* offers you a chance to confront the antagonisms that lurk beneath the surface of our so-called civilized society. It's a rollercoaster ride through the human psyche, where every twist and turn reveals another layer of the onion we call consciousness.

But let's be honest – you're not here for self-improvement. No, you're here for the jouissance, the guilty pleasure of transgression. Each poem is a forbidden fruit, each story a siren song luring you towards the rocks of social taboo. Go ahead, indulge. We won't tell anyone about the shiver of excitement you feel as you thumb through these pages, savoring the delicious wrongness of it all.

And who are the mad geniuses behind this literary Frankenstein's monster? A veritable who's who of the unhinged and brilliant authors: – each one a master of their craft, each one slightly unbalanced in the most delightful way. They've poured their souls onto these pages, and now you get to lap it up like a cat with a saucer of cream laced with LSD.

But here's the kicker, the punchline to this cosmic joke: in the end, it's all contingent. These words, these ideas, this very book – it's all a happy accident, a collision of atoms in the vast emptiness of space. So why not embrace the chaos? Why not dive headfirst into the swirling maelstrom of human experience?

EYEPUBLISHEWE presents this tome not as a mere book, but as a manifesto for the human condition. It's art for humanity's sake, a middle finger to the bland conformity of mainstream literature. This is the underground bubbling up, the id breaking free from the prison of the superego. It's messy, it's raw, it's real – everything that polite society pretends doesn't exist.

So, dear reader, are you brave enough to open this Pandora's box of prose and poetry? To confront the violence hidden beneath the veneer of civility? To stare into the abyss and feel it staring back? If so, then *What is in John's Basement?* awaits you.

But be warned: once you've seen what lurks in those shadowy corners, you can never unsee it. Your rationality will be forever tainted, your worldview forever skewed. You'll walk the streets seeing the Matrix code of ideology everywhere you look. You'll hear the whispers of repressed desires in the rustling of leaves. You'll feel the weight of cosmic insignificance pressing down on you as you contemplate the vastness of space and the inevitability of the worms.

And yet, paradoxically, you'll also feel more alive than ever before. Because in confronting these hidden truths, in embracing the absurdity of existence, you'll find a strange kind of freedom. The freedom to laugh in the face of horror, to find beauty in the grotesque, to dance on the edge of madness.

So come, join us in John's Basement. It's dark down here, but oh so illuminating. Lose yourself in the labyrinth of words, let the prose wash over you like a baptism of fire. Emerge transformed, reborn, ready to see the world through new eyes – eyes that can pierce the veil of rationality and glimpse the chaotic truth beyond.

"What is in John's Basement?" It's you, dear reader. It's all of us. It's the human condition distilled into ink and paper, waiting to be discovered. The only question is: are you ready to face what you'll find down there?

Order now, and remember – in John's Basement, nobody can hear you scream. But they might just hear you laugh.

Tezozomoc is a Los Angeles Chicano Essayist, Poet and 2009 Oscar Nominated Activist, internationally published and has been published by Amoxcalco Books for *I am not your Chihuahua* and by Floricanto Press for *Gashes!: Poems and pain from the halls of injustice,* a collection of poetry (September 2019). He has been featured nationally and internationally across Zoom open virtual mics. Tezozomoc has also been published in the following journals/anthologies: *2021 Boundless Anthology* (January 20, 2022), *MacroMicroCosm, Healing Hands, Vol 7 Issue #3* (April 15, 2021), *Rigorous Journal* (September 21, 2020), *Red Earth Productions & Cultural Work* (December 17, 2019), *Underwood Press* (September 9, 2019), and *Mom Egg Review, Los Angeles Poets for Justice* (March 15, 2021).

"An electric array of poets collected together in this mind-blowing anthology to answer a simple question: What Is In John's Basement? Things appear like they could appear as our intrepid space warriors reveal behind John's basement door. Ghosts and creepy clowns—including Jimbo, trapped forever inside a 'game' of 'Atlantic City,' the ever-present coffee can of rusty nails, blacked out for our protection, Florence Henderson's nightgown, scars and songs, hopes and dreams and always the nightmares, John's basement inside ourselves or far, far beyond fighting The Great Space Worm Invasion. These award-winning writers summoned from exotic corners of the globe dare us to open John's basement door… turn on the light? That's up to you… truth or dare?"

Lee Eric Freedman
Swampscott, Massachusetts Poet Laureate: 2016-2018
Renegade Poet Laureate of Swampscott: 2011-Forever

Truth - took me a while to read your tome . . . I am a smart girl but I don't remember the last time I had to look up so much stuff!
An eclectic group to be sure . . .
Certainly far removed from surveying . . . at least in my mind.
It was quite interesting - kind of like being a pinball bounced from one train of thought to another . . Took me a few sessions - definitely deserves a re-read.

D Diane Wells, Mensa member and Professional Land Surveyor, Southern California

Let's turn to the Book of John's Basement. Chapter: Poker face every God you can find.

Verses: *Karma's a cutthroat card game; Afterlife's calling your bluff; There's a tombstone just awaiting to give you a standing ovation;and Ain't shit you can do about it is yelling from the cheap seats, "Go All IN, bluff the bluff, Death has never had shit to lose!"* Stanzas lifelike like scripture these authors, these daredevils with creativity and diction and tell Life I'll be damned if I lose every time, have come together to prove to the basement of human design we all are emotional high wire acts that love with no safety net. This Eyepublishewe collection is what happens when manna meets every one of y(our) sometimes Life's an hourglass half full of our Makers marks, but I swear if I wake up again tomorrow morning Imma remind our world why being drunk off human is the only thing Life's been willing to die for. A jewel in any collector's collection. *What is in John's Basement* is a reminder to every walking talking breathing miracle's caterpillar(ing) eyes butterflying upon it, that in this card game of life being human is a beautiful gamble, so bet everything that you've collected in **your very own basement**, for whether win or lose, you will always have a tombstone just waiting to give you a standing ovation.

Charles Perry Jr : CP Maze
-2x Individual World Poetry Slam Finalist
Houston, Texas

What is in John's Basement? beckons you into a labyrinth of emotion, mystery, and discovery. Each poem reflects love, loss, humor, and memory, voiced by a diverse array of talents that illuminate the hidden depths of our shared humanity. This anthology pulls you in with its raw honesty and wit, daring you to explore the depths we all carry within. Vivid, moving, and unforgettable, this collection will resonate with anyone who believes in the magic of words and the power of poetry. A must-read for those who seek to be entertained, moved and transformed.

Thomas Open Minds
Freestyle artist, host and founder of a global poetry collective called Open Minds
British Columbia, Canada

"Home to our personal and collective shadows, the basement has long been a cultural fascination and site of mystery. In this diverse anthology, EyePublishEwe's authors explore these depths with suspense, insight, and uncanny humor. Crack the door and enter 'John's Basement:' terrors and treasures await."

Emily Cordes, author of *Queen of Swords* & *Armful of Poppies*

"The first mistake was the need to have space hold contents, now we must realize its many other purposes." So warned and advised the philosopher Henri Lefebvre in his 1974 examination of how we live space, *The Production of Space*. The poets collected in *What is in John's Basement?* firstly know one of the other purposes of space is to free their insights, humor, conjectures, dramatic scenarios, and above all the words that wear the space of their living creativity.

From K.R. Morrison's unique formal device in "Sunder," a seemingly redacted document full of dark 'space' on the page, through Bryan Franco's internalized and externalized meditation on being marked by life, "But my inside scars show themselves through my behavior," to Chiina Bloodmire's echo of Lefebvre's warning, "Askin' what's in this basement, isn't smart you see, my dear... It's the place where I bodied guilt; and fear disappeared..." we take a tour through how poetry absorbs us in its own space of perception and sensation. Many of these poems treat the basement as a kind of primordial mausoleum for angsty humor as in Merilee Johnson's scenario piece with a plot that blends a werewolf anecdote, kookiness of family relationships and a stormy night in the basement. Her poem seems to be in the same genre as Frogg Corpse's list poem of off-kilter Americana whose humor rests in underlying truths of its descriptions about what ends up in a basement. The basement here being one that politics, pop culture, urban myth and satire slowly molder in. The poet hil hoover seems to be Henri Lefebvre's heir when they write, "But where is your joy? or did you (like so many of us) hide it away in boxes and store it in some basement corner in hopes of preserving the pieces to be rifled through on a future date?" There are poems here that work at a sense of space with poignant insights such as Phynne~Belle's "Weight of Absence (a Runway of Lost Chances)," a very personal requiem, lament and memorial melding the spaces of inner life, memory, possibility and regret, with the setting of a daily household. This anthology will host you in many spaces, basements and more liminal zones, that will have you provocatively accommodated the way only great poetry does.

Paul Skiff, a practical artist advocating the re-humanization of culture, NYC

What is in John's Basement? is an often surreal and fascinatingly diverse collection of poetry in various forms and disciplines, tied together very loosely with the string of the thematic title, which rears its head amongst the work of the assembled wordsmiths.

Under the leadership of Commander Cornelius Anne Bigsby III, seemingly a pragmatic leader and retired Fleet Admiral of the Slovakian Navy, the poetry in this collection hints, teases and plays with the potential contents of the aforementioned underground dwelling, sometimes directly and other times as a broad inspiration. The reader is led through a number of storerooms, bunkers, dungeons and labyrinths, revealing shadowy histories, secret gatherings, and barely lit adventures. These are tales of barely hidden blood stains, redacted documents, drugs, sex, music, love, and life, not for the faint of heart or occasionally the easily offended, but constantly engaging and richly rewarding. Well worth exploring.

Aron Smith, Radio presenter, poet, musician
Aberdeen, Scotland

What is in John's Basement?

An eclectic assemblage of prose and poetry

from the out-there minds of mad poets

~nothing to fear at all~

By
Commander Cornelius Anne Bigsby III
Retired Fleet Admiral of the Slovakian Navy

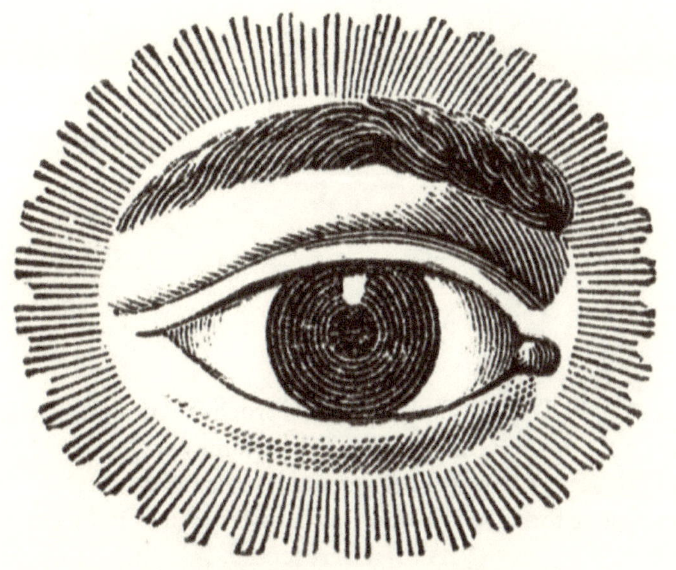

PUBLISH

EYEPUBLISHEWE
PUBLISHING POETRY, LITERATURE, ART, MUSIC
FOR HUMANITY'S SAKE
A BRAND NEW PUBLISHING COMPANY
SAN FRANCISCO
FOUNDED 2020

this book is dedicated

to a mid-century Formica dinette set

TABLE OF CONTENTS

Prologue	xix
What is in John's basement?	23
Sunder	29
Rusty Nails	31
I Have Been Down So Low	32
Because Scars Are Not Japanese Teacups	35
When Night Falls Down The Stairs	39
I see ghosts	41
John's Basement Is In All of Us	42
Atlantic City	46
Call Me Al	50
Singing this song for you - Leon Russell	58
PTSD Odyssey 1985	64
Cinder Cella	65
Answered by What It Is	67
Stormy Night	69
Shifting Shapes	73
The List	75
Dirge of the Vineyard	77
The Real Dream The Real Inquisition	84
What?	90
Why I Am Not a Horror Movie Clown	91
BUSTED	95
Rune	97
The Heat	99
Laughing-Out, Life	101

Depth Charge   103

Empty bed   104

How To Revive   106

Weight of Absence (a Runway of Lost Chances)   108

Cliff Notes for Living on the Edge   111

Fearful Hope Lingers   113

The Sorrowful Shales of Silver Creek   115

Don't worry, dear boy. Have no fear.   117

Epilogue   119

About the Authors   121

About EYEPUBLISHEWE   125

EPE Titles   125

EPE Titles Coming Soon   126

Prologue

In all of history, there are no names that command more reverence and awe than that of Commander Cornelius Anne Bigsby III, a pragmatic leader and retired Fleet Admiral of the Slovakian Navy. Commander Bigsby's exploits are legendary, with unmatched heroism and wisdom. In the words of the Admiral, we recount the horrible prelude to the greatest interstellar horror humanity has ever faced: The Great Space Worm Invasion.

> "Hear me now, brave souls who are carried by fate far beyond this blue marble, this hearth of humanity, our terrestrial home. Heed my words. Out there the cosmos, mostly undiscovered and unmapped, keeps the deadly knowledge and holds it secret, and it dwarfs our understanding of the dire consequences for our way of life. In the autumn of my career, as I was looking out on the unknowable expanse from the bridge of the Nuestra Señora de La Concepción, it was then that fear was struck in what is left of my dead soul as I first witnessed the scavengers setting upon us with glee, our doom being nigh.

> "Now is not the time to regale you with peppershot and rum. They were the interplanetary worms that emerged from the snarling verrucose void, starved with limitless hunger, that knew our feeble minds could neither take account of nor appreciate them. Their segmented bodies shimmered with an eerie bioluminescence, twisting and writhing while they advanced upon our outposts. These creatures, born in the darkest corners of the universe, possessed an intelligence that belied their monstrous forms.

"Initially, to say that we were fraught with peril is laughably apt. With lost ships and colonies decimated, our hope waned. Yet, in the face of this nightmare, this terrible adversity, we refused to submit to their slimy intention. We would not be overwhelmed. Our spirits shone brighter than Procyon. We made do as good sailing warriors do. What an education! We fought and will fight on.

"Prepare yourselves, for the invasion is upon us. And in the famous words of Silver Star recipient and deckhand Skip Farkaš, 'We will swab decks in hell before we hit the racks to sleep!' Although he was anally executed by a sky crawler in '73, his resilience in the fight kept his balls afloat, and with his spirit, it'll keep your Slovak sacs swimming upright to battle these slimy gunta looking motherfuckers from ass-eating your families.

"As we stand on the precipice of this new era, let us remember the sacrifices of those who came before us. Let their courage be our guide, their determination our shield. The worms are not merely a threat to our existence; they are a threat to our freedoms. We will pile drive those tubular fucks back into their dingy dwelling shell holes!

"There's one thing you will be able to say when this war is over and you get back home. Thirty years from now, when you're sitting by your fireside with your grandson farting on your fucking knee and he asks, 'What did you do in the Great War?' you won't have to cough and say, 'Well, your gran shoveled shit in Bratislava.' No sir, you can look 'em straight in the eye and say, 'Son, I rode with the great Navy and a son of a bitch named Admiral Bigsby.'

"We will win this war. We will show those worms we have more guts than they have or ever will have! There is no way we are just going to shoot the bastards and call it even. They will have their goddamned living guts ripped out and used as boot polish. We're going to murder those lousy bilateral cocksuckers from Khambalia to fucking Kung Pao."

What is in John's basement?
(Uh, do we want to go there?)

By John Angell Grant

And find, perhaps (just sayin')
Sex; theft; betrayed girlfriends;
stolen objects.
Old broken bicycles,
broken toys,
broken hearts,
maybe even neglected bits of body parts,
lying around
that you forgot to throw
in the bag
and get to the dumpster
before the police came.

Wait a minute.
Maybe we don't want to go down this road.

What about a happy basement poem?

For example, there's the kayak
we can bring out in July
For a river run.
And a couple of inner tubes for the kids.

There's an electric scooter.
(What is that doing in the basement?
That should be out on the front porch.)

This is confusing.
The basement is a place
Where you throw things
you don't want to look at,
But you can't decide
What to do with them.

Then you tip-toe down
the stairs
a few years later,
After your relative has died,
and you're a horrified to find
not just the silver coin box,
but also a thumb,
Or what looks like a thumb
From a human being.
What!?

Should I call the police?

I've never written a police poem before.
I mean, we all have our share
of horror stories,
right?
How much is your life
defined by horror stories,
and how much is defined
by good things that happened to you?

Commander Cornelius Anne Bigsby III

For me,
I had one good parent,
and one damaged parent,
So I have some of this,
and some of that.

Which leaves us
With both "a basement,"
and "abasement."

When I lift up the lid
of the wooden box
(not the silver box!)
it doesn't smell good.
So I close the lid of the wooden box.
And that's the way it is.
If you want to take a look
inside
bring a pair of gloves.

The basement is
dark.
I fumble around.

What is in John's Basement?

Yesterday when I attempted the steps
downward
I stubbed my foot and fell.
The darkness rushed up at me.
In recent years,
I've lost that "proprioception" thing
that provides balance.
Do you know that word?
"Proprioception?"
When functioning,
It allows me to feel
three things:
first, my body parts in their location;
second, those same body parts during their motion,
and third, the same body parts
during the intention of their actions.

Unfortunately,
No more.
the proprioception is gone.

The problem is, I'm aging.
My feet are numb from the neuropathy
Of dying nerves.
So I'm down to just one sense:
my eyes.

But in the dark,
Eyes are not helpful.
and with the proprioception gone,
and the sensation in my feet gone,
I'm in freefall;

Commander Cornelius Anne Bigsby III

though I'm not sure
what's going on,
because nothing is hitting me
as I drop
in free fall

So am I falling,
or am I sitting still and imagining
I'm falling?
It's difficult to tell
down here
in the basement today.

And also I see now
that there is
a sub-basement.
What happens when I blast
through the basement
into the sub-basement below?
Do I travel,
eventually,
down to the other side of the world,
and come up,
at some point,
in, say,
a basement
in Laos?

Then go
up a set of stairs
to a sunny place
on the other side of the world?

What is in John's Basement?

Because here I am on the other side,
right now,
In the sun.

So what's in John's basement?
It turns out to be
Old stuff
That I can toss;
Or keep;
Or give away.
Would you like that
silver coin box?

Commander Cornelius Anne Bigsby III

Sunder

By K.R. Morrison

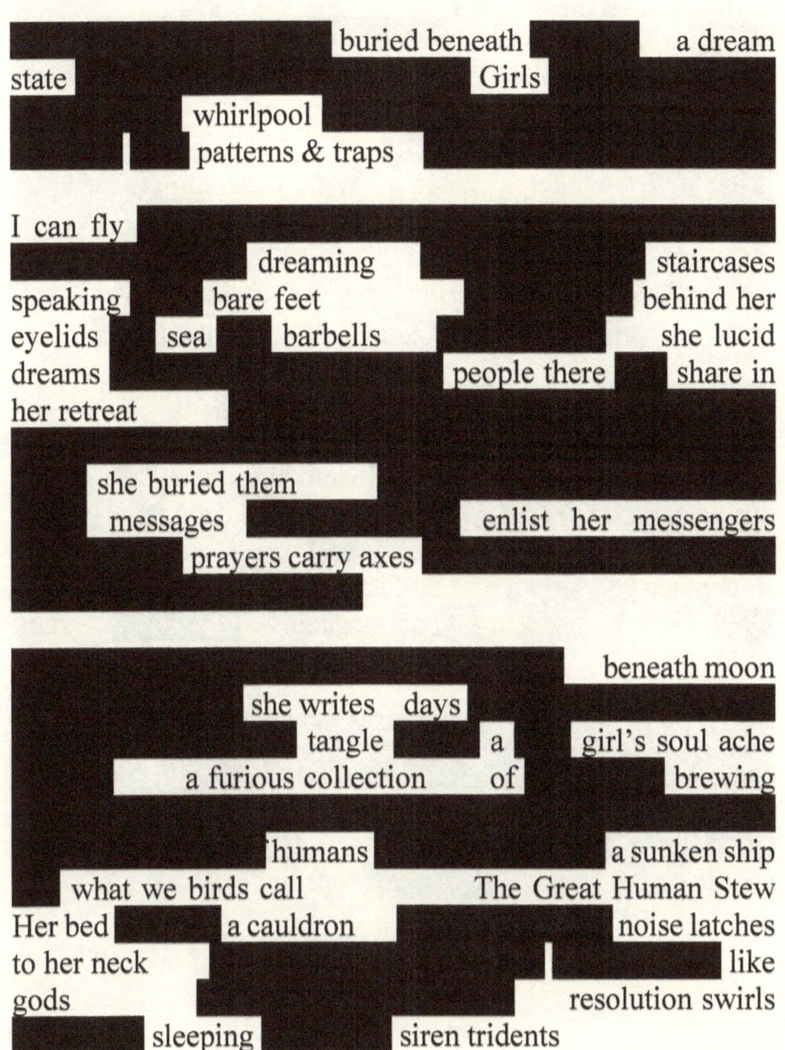

What is in John's Basement?

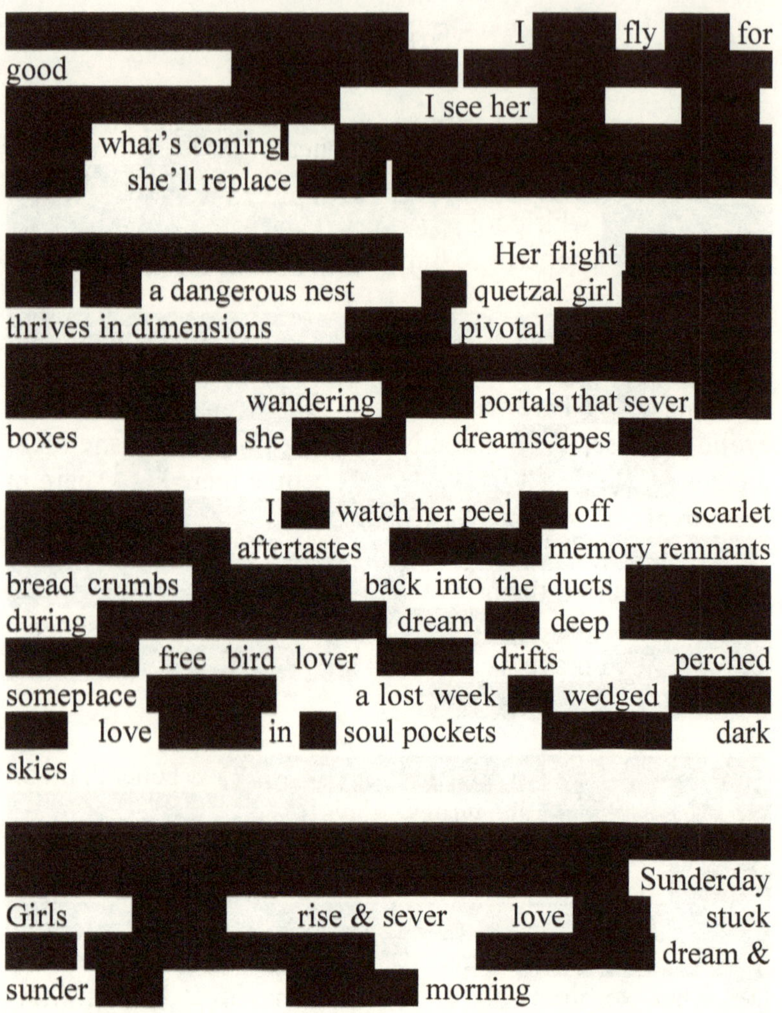

Commander Cornelius Anne Bigsby III

Rusty Nails
By Dane Ince

A lonely wrench resting deeply for a while in darkness the job left unfinished

A coffee can full of rusty nails yet another thing completely left undone

In the solid silent shadows the boiler squawked a creepy monolog while water pipes witnessed

A lonely wrench resting deeply for a while in darkness the job left unfinished

What is in John's Basement are parts and pieces of lives diminished

The mystery of memories of ghosts of long ago Saturdays that were fun

A lonely wrench resting deeply for a while in darkness the job left unfinished

A coffee can full of rusty nails yet another thing completely left undone

I Have Been Down So Low
The Ground Looked Up

By Ron Whitehead

I have been down so low the ground looked up.
Failure has been my greatest success.

Failure has been my best teacher.
I learned to listen to my failures and grow.

Daddy was a bare knuckle boxer,
the fiercest of them all.

He never lost a fight.
He taught me how to take a punch,

and then another, always watching
for the opening, then fast as lightning

jab jab jab with the left,
then with the right fast as lightning go kaboom.

Daddy was a boxer.
He taught me how to be a warrior, how to fight.

He taught me how to fight through pain,
ignoring blood, sweat, and tears,

to never give up, no matter what,
to keep fighting, even in pain. So I became a boxer.

Unlike Daddy I have lost more fights
than I have won. But Daddy taught me

to never give up and that life won't always be fun.
You ask, "Why did you fail so many times?"

And I say, "Because I have always stubbornly
chosen to go my own damn way, to be a rebel poet,

Commander Cornelius Anne Bigsby III

to adventure places where no one I know
had ever gone." So time and time and time again

I failed. I hit rock bottom with nowhere left to go.
Many times I have stood alone,

abandoned by everyone, but Mama.
She never left my corner of the ring.

Even when I hadn't seen or heard
from her in ages I knew she was always there.

So every time I failed I remembered
how Daddy and Mama had grown up,

the challenges they faced and overcame,
while keeping their resolve

and maintaining strong good attitudes.
So when I found myself

fallen so low the ground looked up,
I went to a place I came to call ground zero.

I remembered that I left the farm
when I was seventeen and I was on my own.

There was only me carrying a few clothes
in a backpack and a small suitcase. That's where I start

to build myself anew and live again.
Slowly, determinedly, taking one step at a time,

I find ways to rise again,
and build my life anew.

I am now seventy-three years of age,
a rocky rugged scarred poet,

a gentle soul, the wild nature
Kentucky farm boy I always was.

Now I have grown old.
Miles and miles I have traveled

What is in John's Basement?

to here and there and everywhere
my heart whispered to go go go.

Many fights I have fought
in my ragged life

and despite all the losses,
and against all the odds,

relentlessly leaning into the howling winds
I still stand strong.

And without regrets I remain the boxer poet
writing poems I discover every step along the way

.

Commander Cornelius Anne Bigsby III

Because Scars Are Not Japanese Teacups

By Bryan Franco

When I was 49, I tripped on
my front stairs and fell into a bush.

I had a cut across my forehead
that quickly scabbed over.
(Luckily, there was no scar.)

It amazed me how many people
asked me about my injury which
wasn't an awful injury.

When I was a kid, my mom
taught me it was rude to ask
people about injuries and scars.

So I told people I was bungee jumping
from the Casco Bay Bridge and
bumped my head on a girder.

When I was six, I was
running downstairs
as six-year-olds do.

I was carrying a freshly-sharpened pencil
when I tripped over my feet
as six-year-olds do.

What is in John's Basement?

At that moment, as
my body tumbled, my
handheld tight to the
freshly-sharpened pencil,
which found its way into
the skin above my knee.

It did not draw blood, but
left a small blue dot that
still exists to this day.
It's a scar in the form of a tattoo.

When I was 8, I acquired
a small ¾-inch diagonal scar on
my right wrist when I fell off my bike.

Several months after my
mother passed away, I
was unpacking a box
of her stuff that was
now my stuff.

I carefully swiped a box cutter along the top
of a box when it slipped from the packing
tape to the top end of my left forearm.
I became the proud recipient of a
two-inch keloid souvenir.

Those scars are surface scars, scars
that only serve as memories of
inconsequential incidents.

Commander Cornelius Anne Bigsby III

When people ask me how
the forearm scar happened,
I tell them it happened during
a hang-gliding mishap, then I tell
them the truth.

But the scars I worry most about are invisible.
They exist inside my psyche.
They exist a history.
They exist as trauma.
They exist as reasons to see a therapist.
They exist as poetry.
They exist abstract art with what has
been called primitive brushstrokes.
To me, taping a canvas to create clean lines
doesn't reflect the way life works.
Sometimes, our traumas are
what makes us better people.
It's true that we can react to trauma
by taping our future decisions to
create even lines and shapes, but
my reality tends to lean askew.

The blue dot is still there but has faded
and shrunk in relation to my adult size.
The scar on my wrist is barely visible.
The box-cutter scar is as pronounced
as the veins that rise from my wrist.

But my inside scars show themselves
through my behavior.

What is in John's Basement?

My inside scars play hide-and-seek in
my sleeping dreams.

I cannot cover them with make-up or clothing.

I can only learn to exist with them each next
time they come up for air by learning how
to recognize when they will surface.

I could try to lay down figurative
tape to straighten them out, but
their rough edges will still exist.

Because I can't kintsugi them with liquid gold
or a facsimile I buy at a craft store, I welcome
them as part of my whole, so when they
come up for air, they don't have to grab
their Albuterol inhalers, then they can
breathe easy so I can breathe easy.

Commander Cornelius Anne Bigsby III

When Night Falls Down The Stairs

By Deborah C. Segal

In the basement is a prison of memories, and it grew in your mind the world wasn't real, only an idea. And, like a virus it was contagious. You tell yourself what you already knew, like an infinite staircase—you can't exist in the real world!

It was dark when you carved a path down. There, you see the abyss transcends the basement. You wonder, have I gone to the abyss, or gone nuts? How to drop a belief in reality, without gravity? What does one sense or feel, and not just know? You had locked something away deep inside: the truth that one can break free.

What the human mind conceives is contagious. Reminders of what exists in the basement, when the infinite staircase is viewed from the inside! One glance may drive normal people nuts.

At the top step was a simple idea: you can't die in a dream at rock bottom. & as the notion grew, this world is not real, and there is no rock bottom, because a person who never gets out of the basement, doesn't know!

Norman Bates' mummified mom is in the basement, and a Ouija board & Voodoo doll pin cushion, & the basement is a nightmare factory for nuts, rodents, snakes, and bats when darkness comes inside.

What is in John's Basement?

Embalm the misunderstood cryptid from inside! The broken scalpel doesn't work, and old John the Baker is always lurking among the fruit and nuts.

What's that smell? Why's it so dark down here? Did that cryptid move? Don't you know? Destroy the mutant creature. Gestate the monster from the inside where it is gripped by the spirit of the night, where it will dig deep in the moist trenches.

Oh, let this be the spirit of the times: Contagious! Nightmares! Rock Bottom!
Caged cryptids hissing in the basement will integrate the shadow in a heartbeat

Commander Cornelius Anne Bigsby III

I see ghosts
By Mbonisi Zikhali Zomkhonto

I see ghosts in every turn, lanterns discovered in the thick of dark, glooming underneath several millennia of doom. I have seen my late grandfather wielding a shield and red teeth, from colonialism punching him in the jaw. I used to think I was mad seeing him there, rocking back and forth, watching me like I stole his right to live. One day I saw him on my plate. As if he wanted me to have red teeth from eating him raw. He asked politely, eat my death with pride and there is more of me hidden in the grave. because I never rotted away like a coward, and I know you were raised carnivore.

John's Basement Is In All of Us

By Mark States

Certainly, over the decades this basement has seen more than its fair share
of rough-hewn faces
the down & outs, the down & inconsolable:
Depression-era migrants needing a place to rest their heads
while searching for the next odd job and next meal;
war veterans who've witnessed too many mangled bodies of friends,
and washing their minds with alcohol only serve
to mangle their own lives even further.
Every single one clinging to the taint of the American Dream
fretting which fetid rabbit hole they were facing –
and never getting a piece of the American Pie.

This basement eventually might see a leaning tower of pizza boxes
and lounging sunglass-wearing cockroaches content after feast of leftover crusts
while "Sonny" is on his latest 24-hour bender –
bent over keyboard and joystick:
master of Grand Theft Auto
pawn of Grandma McNarcissist

Commander Cornelius Anne Bigsby III

But no, this film is black & white, and John toots a party favor
in front of his basement door.
One might find this setting appropriate
for a Rod Serling intro to a Twilight Zone episode,
a portal to a bizarre new world, a twist of fate or circumstance,
a commentary on the perversity of post-modern capitalism.
What in the world is in John's basement? And why is John
on such a mild-altering drugs display of excitement,
eager to show it off?
That one of John's personal demons
is off camera on a smoke break, should be enough of a clue –
a red flag if his world were not black & white –
that what you are stepping into is not an episode of television
but of paranoid hallucinatory schizophrenia.

I've watched too many episodes of Criminal Minds
the torture rooms, trails of dismembered bodies,
the mazes of broken glass and dead-end hopes,
too many rooms where you check in for one night and then
"check out' permanently.

I've watched too many poets on my computer and they all
speak to me.
They are looking right at me and no one is behind me. It HAS
to be me!

What is in John's Basement?

Rich Boucher and his new power drill are still fresh in my mind.
It's not so much the cranium shavings he is gently caressing off
my face,
nor the blood splatter he's wiping off his,
what really hurts is that I thought we were friends.
Perhaps we still are and I just do not realize it,
too triggered by my own experience to understand
how much he cares about what is happening to me.

I've howled with glee watching Hitman stand over booby-
trapped bathtub
telling that Boris Bad Enough guy
"Yell all you like – the Lord himself won't hear you"

I've watched the blitzkrieged minds of our generation
crumble into gritty dust – like broken shells on a beach under
the weight of
internet conspiracy videos and podcasts
peddling fears that political parties are running child porn rings
from the basements and back rooms of New Jersey pizza
parlors
and creating viral microchips in the basements of clandestine
medical research centers
and plotting to take away your guns and the right to say stupid
shit
in supersecret meetings held in their luxurious illuminati
penthouses
which the elite won't tell you are really basements
(if you turn the building upside down) because they want to
keep you

Commander Cornelius Anne Bigsby III

in the dark about the roof
the real roof that will set you free
and the only way to save yourself is to click on that Subscribe
button
and don't forget to buy their merch and …
by golly, a lot of these podcasts are created in people's
basements, so …
yeah, a lot of skanky stuff goes on in basements …

Do I really need to know what is in John's basement?
I'm not dying to know.
Nor am I dying because I found out!
Naw, I'm good.
Take a whack at it yourself if you want.
There is nothing to lose except everything.

Atlantic City

By Jeff Cottrill

They're dragging me to prison again.

That's the way it goes, here in Atlantic City. I came here young and naïve, expecting a gambling paradise, and found myself in a police state. There's never a warning, never a chance to escape, not even a questioning from the authorities or from those who accuse you. They don't even tell you what your alleged crime is. They grab you and haul you straight to the city's only jail facility.

Mind you – it's not so bad once you're there. Prisoners in Atlantic City are permitted visitors anytime, with no limit. And they still allow you to collect *some* of your work earnings. Not your regular base salary; that gets delayed until they let you out. Sometimes they let you out right away, if you have the funds to pay the proper fine, or if you flash a special card. Sometimes you can get out early if you play along and, shall we say, roll the dice right. Typically, though, you stay incarcerated for a given amount of time and then get out. And you think you're free – but you never are. Because they'll get you again. They'll drag you off, and the whole routine plays out as before. It's maddening and absurd. An American Kafka tale. But that's how it is here.

For years, I've yearned to escape Atlantic City. But I can't. It's an endless cycle in which you travel around the city, over and over, along the same route, seeing the same streets, the same railroads, and none of them ever change, and you can't leave, and you never find a true home. Sure, the streets are colourful,

Commander Cornelius Anne Bigsby III

as are the buildings on them – but they're all surrounded by a drab grey that never goes away. Where are all the casinos? you ask yourself. Where are the glitz and the glamour? Were these only a myth designed to entrap us all? Oh, there's plenty of *money* here. I can confirm that. Atlantic City is a rich place full of opportunity. But it's a cutthroat one. Invest well, and you can come out on top, and you rarely have to pay taxes. Find yourself on the wrong street and you can be decimated in less than a blink – depending on who owns the street and what they've built there.

They're crazy about real estate in this town. That seems to be the only game around. You can purchase whole avenues at shockingly low prices – sixty, a hundred, two hundred bucks! You can buy national railroads and even the City utilities if you get to them before anyone else does, or if they get auctioned off. And the rentals can bring in good cash on the side – especially when you start building homes and accommodations. But Atlantic City has authoritarian methods of collecting these rentals for investors. If they catch you loitering on a competitor's street, they'll make you pay rent for *being* there. That's not so bad – usually just a few bucks – until the houses and hotels start going up, and then you have to be careful. I went through a rough spot not long ago, when I was stuck on the Boardwalk, and the only place to stay was that great red hotel. They charged me two thousand dollars, just for one night. Two thousand. And I had no choice. It could have plunged me into instant bankruptcy.

How lucky I had my own property as a backup. It was devastating, though. I had to sell all of my houses on Kentucky, Indiana and Illinois Avenues at half-price, and then I had to mortgage those same streets. I barely collected enough. Thank God I received my regular salary right after I left the Boardwalk – and then, by Chance, they dragged me off to prison again, for no conceivable reason. That's the funniest thing about Atlantic City: sometimes, jail is a haven. You can relax and avoid the unpredictable pitfalls of this real-estate market. Who knows what might have happened to me if I hadn't been safe in jail, still free to collect rent on my own property. I might have stepped on the wrong spot again and been knocked out of the game for keeps.

Don't get me wrong – there are other ways to make money in this town, but they're infrequent and unreliable. There are opera nights and Xmas funds. There's the occasional beauty contest. (I came in second place once and received ten dollars; I never found out what the first prize was.) If you're lucky, you can get a couple of hundred dollars when there's a bank error in your favour. You might get money when your building and loan matures. I once received a dividend of fifty bucks, although I can't remember buying any corporate shares.

Some of these side income sources seem shady and dubious indeed. There's that free parking spot in the middle of town. I don't know what's going on there, but every time I park my car there, the parking attendant gives me money. Five hundred dollars in cash. Hands it to me as if it's the most normal thing in the world. *But what for?* I ask him. *Where is this money coming from?* He never tells me. Just smiles and walks away. And I take the money every time, but something feels wrong about it. Even by the twisted logic of this town, it seems like something... outside of the rules.

Commander Cornelius Anne Bigsby III

I avoid parking there these days. Who knows what dirty scheme they're involved in.

Dear God, how I wish I could leave Atlantic City. After years of roaming here, of making and losing money so randomly, I've come to find it the most boring and meaningless place in existence. I dream of other lives. Surely I could have been anything else. A pair of ragged claws? Or perhaps I could have been a world conqueror, dominating nations from Argentina to Kamchatka. Or I could have been a sleuth, solving murders in great mansions. Or an island settler, building roads and settlements in exchange for sheep and wood. Or a navy captain, sinking cruisers and submarines with well-aimed missiles. A simple rail passenger. A dungeon master. A surgeon with hands so skilled that the instruments never touch the sides of the incisions. I could have been a hippo. I swear – I'd be willing to transform into a hippopotamus living on nothing but giant white marbles, to get out of this town for a day. Why, Lord? Why such a cruel fate?

What's this? I'm free again? Looks like Chance has intervened once more, and I'm spared another brief prison term. I suppose I'll make a brief pit stop at the water works. Today, they're charging me a whopping one hundred and twenty dollars – just to wander around the plant. It's absurd. But that's the way things go here.

Someday, I may make it out of Atlantic City. Until then... please keep a bed free for me at Marvin Gardens.

What is in John's Basement?

Call Me Al

By Michael Sindler

You wake up. You're in a bed that's not your own.
"It's o.k." you think, "I'm on the road. I'm not supposed to be at home".

You look around. This place is grungy...really grungy. The bed looks like you were just the last of many who had slept there since the sheets had been changed. You pick at a nasty, crusty dried puddle of something and hope it's not what you think it is. How the hell did you get here?

You remember being in the Port Authority bus station. You look around and don't see your bag anywhere. Not a good sign. Thinking back (which is hard because your head is splitting) you remember getting off the bus and going into the terminal. You remember calling Jane and telling her you would catch an Uber over to her apartment.

Looking around again at the concrete block walls, painted some sort of "used-to-be-green" tone speckled with what appears to be mold, you know this is definitely NOT Jane's place. She lives in a nice Chelsea brownstone on the third floor. You've seen pictures of it. Neat and homey and drenched in sunlight. This place doesn't have a window, not one. You're sure it's not the third floor of anything and especially not Jane's 28th Street brownstone. You see that the door is metal, painted battleship gray and displaying three deadbolt locks in addition to the one on the doorknob.

Commander Cornelius Anne Bigsby III

"Where the fuck am I?" you ask yourself.

At least you aren't naked or in restraints. You fight terror with faux humor. Not much to be thankful for but something. A tiny, tiny thing. How is it a thing at all? What does it prove? Hopefully nothing too bad has happened. You don't feel any signs of being abused or violated. Still, your stomach tightens up. You have your bra and panties and t-shirt on. You see your jeans lying on the floor and your jacket hanging off a pathetic excuse for a coffee table made of four orange milk crates and an old wooden door. Jesus fucking Christ-- what have you gotten yourself into? Think... think...

The bus station. You were starving. You grabbed P-nut butter crackers, some so-called "trail" mix, and an awful tasting energy drink from the vending machines. You were sore and tired from the long trip from Canfield. You called for the Uber, told them you were at the bus station and were told to wait outside on 42nd street and the driver would call when he was close and describe the vehicle he was in. You took an escalator down and followed signs to get to the 42nd street exit. It wasn't really cold but the breeze and the energy of all the people pushing past you, many focused on their phones as they floated through the river of bodies coursing along the sidewalk in both directions, the currents intermingling. The rush made you zip your jacket up and pull the collar tight.

You waited for what seemed like an hour, but was actually just twenty-five minutes. You stood in front of the building trying not to block the doorway or get sucked into the riptide of the sidewalk stream. You remember the Uber driver calling and telling you he would be in a maroon Ford Mini-van. He told you he would be there within five minutes. Ten minutes later a van rolled up fitting the description and honking its horn. A chunky white guy with a sleeve tattoo of a snake wrapping around and around his arm and shades sitting atop his balding head waved toward you as the y automatic door opened. Grabbing your bag, you made your way through the crowd, zig-zagging to keep from knocking into someone or being knocked down yourself. Throwing your bag in ahead of you, you jumped as the door slowly closed again, making a scraping noise as its mechanism ground against the frame.

The first thing you noticed was the smell... a mélange of some sort of Asian food, cigarette smoke and the body odor of the driver, whose name was Al (of course it was. So many Uber drivers seemed to be named Al. A coincidence?)

"Call me Al" he said. "Just like the song" and gave a creepy smile showing too much teeth while chuckling at his own lame joke he had no doubt used a million times. "So- 28th and 6th Ave, eh? Nice neighborhood. I got some pals live not far away" he said, You nodded, not really wanting to get engaged in a conversation if you could help it.

Commander Cornelius Anne Bigsby III

He took off and you got your first taste of NYC traffic. It was a rude awakening because there seemed to be no respect for any traffic law you remembered and seemingly every single driver was laying on their horn. When you saw this on TV or in the movies you thought it was overdone but, damn, it was just as bad or worse than you could have imagined.

 "I got some bottled water in da' coola' if youse thousty," Al said in a comically thick accent that seemed SO "Noo Yawk" you almost started laughing.
Looking down at the floor, you saw a large blue igloo cooler with a white hinged top. You couldn't help but also notice that this was the dirtiest, most unkempt Uber you had ever been in. Wrappers and various other trash were strewn about the floor and the seat you were on and (as you craned a bit to look back and see) noticeable heaps of it on the seat behind you, which had cardboard boxes stacked precariously upon it. You were sure they were going to tumble and fall as Al drove maniacally downtown towards your destination.
You opened the cooler, which was filled with a dozen or so plastic Poland Spring water bottles floating in a half-melted pool of ice and water. Screwing the top off you guzzled the water down, realizing just how parched and dehydrated you felt. You finished it in two gulps, then reached back into the cooler for a second one, drinking it just a little slower, and then pouring the last ounce or so onto your hand (dripping a little onto the dirty floorboard) and rubbing it on your face and neck, then swabbing it off with your jacket sleeve.

What is in John's Basement?

It felt good to wipe away the sweat and grime and made you feel like you were rubbing Ohio itself away. For the first time really feeling that you were actually here in the Big Apple, you looked out the window as you alternately zipped by or sat (stuck in traffic) in front of all manner of storefronts, some familiar and many totally new to you - dazzling and exotic. You started to feel the stress and strain and weariness of your voyage across the Midwest and the Northeast via Greyhound, stuck in that seat that was surely ergonomically designed to cause the most discomfort possible. You felt yourself getting tired and impatient, wishing the traffic was as light as back home so you could get to Jane's, take a shower, throw on some sweats and take a quick nap before going out to eat something you could never find at home and see the lights of Broadway or whatever adventure Jane had planned.

 Your eyelids started to droop and you found yourself jerking your chin up repeatedly, opening your eyes and realizing you had dozed off a little. Hopefully you hadn't snored, you thought, though it didn't really matter that much to you if Al heard you honk and wheeze a little bit as you made your way half-conscious towards Chelsea. You felt yourself getting more and more tired and your arms feeling like they were hanging off of you about to drop like overripe fruit from your shoulders onto the floor of the Mini-van. And then there was nothing.

Commander Cornelius Anne Bigsby III

You didn't remember anything after that point, not until just moments ago when you woke up on this creaking, worn mattress covered by these disgusting stained sheets in this ugly cinderblock box of a room.

"Oh shit!" you think to yourself, "this is bad, really bad."

Tears drop down onto the sheets as you scan around for your phone. You make your way onto your feet, feeling groggy, weak, and disoriented and reach down to pick up your pants and grab your jacket. You search all the pockets for your phone, but it's not there. You look desperately over every surface, under the bed and table, but no luck. There's no trace of your bag whatsoever, nor any of its contents. You pull your dirty jeans on, and only at that moment does it occur to you that your shoes are gone as well.

"Bad... really bad... really fucking bad" you tell yourself, spiraling into full-on panic.

You make your way to the door, the bare linoleum floor cold and sticky under your bare feet. You try to turn the handle. It's locked. You knew it would be. The panic continues to build. You're shaking, and your chest is tightening. You try to door again. It won't budge. You pull at it with no effect except making your already painful arms ache more. You knock and knock against the grey metal surface. Your knocks progress into pounding and slapping until your knuckles start to bleed and you can barely wiggle your fingers.

"Please, please, please, please, please" you moan between sobs, wiping away tears and leaving bloodstains in their place from your scraped and cut fingers. "Please, let me out. Please, I have to go to Chelsea. I have to get out. Please let me out"
 You scream until your throat is hoarse. Nothing but silence from outside the door.
And then...

The unmistakable sound of a needle being dropped on a vinyl record.

For a brief moment, there is the sound of static and scratching as the disk spins. And then a song starts to play, a familiar "classic rock" song from the 80's made even more familiar by recent events. A happy strumming guitar lays down a groove that in a different situation would be infectious. A funky bassline and syncopated percussion join in. Then the vocalist with his unmistakable thin tenor begins to sing. You know these words. A chill goes up your spine and spreads throughout your body as the verse moves into the chorus...

"If you'll be my bodyguard I can be your long lost pal. I can call you Betty. And Betty, when you call me...You can call me Al. You can call me Al!"

Commander Cornelius Anne Bigsby III

You drop to your knees, shaking and sobbing hysterically. Tears, spittle, phlegm, and blood mix as you hold your hands to your face, gently rapping your forehead against the door, at first without rhythm but slowly finding yourself matching the beat as the needle is picked up and put down again repeatedly in the same groove. You wish and hope and pray to anyone and anything to get you out of here, to get you to Jane's, to get you to your parents' old familiar safe home back in Canfield-- anywhere other than here behind this door in this cold green moldy room.

You beat your head harder and harder and harder against the obstacle blocking your way. Now your forehead is bleeding, the viscous warm fluid flowing down your face, into your eyes and blinding you. You beat harder and harder but nothing happens, nothing changes. Just the repetition of that one line blaring from the unseen sound system...

"You can call me Al. You can call me Al. You can call me Al. You can call me Al. You can call me Al. You can call me Al..."

What is in John's Basement?

Singing this song for you - Leon Russell

By Antoinette Vella Payne

Dissonant screech
in every melodic backdrop
sung by ghosts.
"Life is strife", they say,

Doing karaoke as the
dungeon floor falls into an abyss,
over ripe plums dripping like
skulls sliced width wise.

Ambulances cry out
in early morning mist.
It's the nature of addiction.
Find the fix fill the hole

Mend the need to
make us whole.
Bodies varied,
Gaining strength of mind

Faltering at the finish line.
All versions condensed to one,
like cells dying then renewed
we remain the same.

Seduced by legal tender,
flamingo feathers strutting bare,
ravaged by alcohol, age & cigarettes.
Chasing green in a slot machine.

Commander Cornelius Anne Bigsby III

Around the curb,
Flowers bring kindness out in everyone.
Exulted sweet souls reign,
We chortle, chuckle, crackle, laugh.

After years in the grave,
gin boosted from juniper berries,
fermented like formaldehyde with
enough water to stay afloat.

Wandering this world--
Airport to boat dock.
Your vessel of choice
heading for distant black holes,

Unseen nor heard.
Pulsing in sync with
shooting stars or
God's breath calling

Creation's creatures
Twin designs--fruit flies & jelly fish,
built like humans.
Mouth to bowel.

Desert winds bluster bold.
Ride me home with
Leon Russell singing
this song for you—

What is in John's Basement?

And I take it.
Like an ogre,
grotesque in my mind
singing like the seraphim,

Dancing like a bull.
Light on my feet
With a sway.
My talents unclaimed,

Standing in the ocean,
waves & wind dripping
down my face
in sheer gratitude for solitude.

Summer sizzled before the
marine layer made moss
mild enough to brush away,
yet the taste lingers.

Children learn rhymes,
changing a line here & there
to fit the times.
Eenie meenie mineee mo

Lit a match
to a snail,
Schizophrenia lurked in
tart grapes budding on the vine.

Commander Cornelius Anne Bigsby III

We ate them anyway,
Letting go of guilt
every time we reach for dopamine
over any good reason.

Compassion the prize
for me & for you.
Strength & grace
Dynamic duo.

Under the cracked engine block,
seeping transmission fluid
onto wooden planks
resembling blood

Stained brown paper bags &
stripped shiny soup cans,
homes for long nails & short black tacks
waiting for their glory day.

Sure of purpose
Given to narcissist hammer,
Pounding out pleasure
Neurotransmitters offering a punch

Under passive pressure
Government laws & lies,
Twisting truth made up to suit
some acceptable history line.

What is in John's Basement?

John's basement,
surrounded by this fascist, racist state
storing tools for the taking by
everyone who will someday belong.

Jehovah Shalom
LORD of peace
name of God
when there was no peace in Israel,

Gaza was destroyed
while the world watched
and Leon Russell sang
this song for you,

On the radio,
proof of invisible tidings.
Air waves where
seagulls float.

And tiny Yemen calls
U.S, U.K. & Israel foreign
terrorists choosing
whether I live or not.

Part of you as part of me
sharing destiny.
Eclipsing our special identity &
Leon Russell's ghost sings his song

Commander Cornelius Anne Bigsby III

On the radio
in the background
of this distant time
mapping space & dividing up eternity-

What is in John's Basement?

PTSD Odyssey 1985

By Jonathan S. Baker

Once a week
on Saturday at one,
the county tests
the tornado sirens
blaring for miles
blaring for a minute
and Odysseus throws
his Pabst smashing
against the wall
of the television room.
Penelope knows
he can't help it,
but still she shakes.
Her hands tremble at the loom.
Seeing her discomfort as disgust
her husbands nerves turn to anger.
He turns on her.
Yelling,
Cunt!
Bitch!
Whore!
Until both their screams
blare through the home.
and Telemachus
climbs out his bedroom window
and runs to the edge
of the property
where the dog is buried
and cries hoping til dark
hoping when they notice his absence
the sirens will end.

Commander Cornelius Anne Bigsby III

Cinder Cella

By Chiina Bloodmire

Le Twist, My Kingdom; carved from flesh and bone,
Down there, beneath the brick and stone,
Holds our basement of secret thrones,
Where we dress our foes...
In lace... to set the tone,
Immortal Sound croonin' in the background... to drown out
their groans...
Cuz down here we dance with muthafuckas who thought they
could go... Toe to Toe...
Cloaked; in elegance, as the legends unfold,
I wove; their end with threads of gold,
Kept their screams in jars I still hold...

Welcome to my Cinder Cella,
Their final breaths; a hauntin' novella...

Down here, under the glamour and charm,
Where 12am... was never an alarm,
I took my pen, and a dagger, long and warm,
Ink became poison, blade not subtle.. I'm tryna harm...
Them... Write their endings, as quiet as a storm...

See, my basement ain't like others you know,
No broken lamps or dust just for show,
Every light lit, by a soul; I once let go,
Cobwebs spun from the lies; They Wilber slow,
Till I caught 'em... under the moon's low glow...

What is in John's Basement?

Their execution became a scene...
Gold chandeliers; glistenin' as they dangle from these beams,
Reflections flicker; in mirrors...
As I sway to the rhythm; of their muffled screams...
In my enchanted realm, no one hears your pleas....

Cinderella got glass shoes, but me?
I walk on skulls, Timbs tappin' with glee,
I heel toe on their graves, leave 'em full of debris,
While the ink from my quill fed on their dreams,
No fairy tale here, just been raw doggin' destiny...
Gave her that good head, so both her and Karma move for
me...
So every time you fuck up, we follow up in 3s...

Askin' what's in this basement, isn't smart you see, my dear...
It's the place where I bodied guilt; and fear disappeared...
Where souls I've captured echo against these walls... New
victims wallow, knowin' their end is near...
Hummin' lullabies only I can hear...

Lady Bloodmire don't play games,
I feast on the wicked, feed on their false claims,
Turn their skeletons into picture frames,
Hang them high with no guilt... no shame...
For they are to blame...

So here's the truth, from deep down below,
Where secrets fester and true colors show,
Every foe I've faced now reaps what they sow,
I let them rest in the glow they don't know,
For this basement is mine—and I run the show...

-End Scene

Commander Cornelius Anne Bigsby III

Answered by What It Is

By John Burroughs

Hettie Jones and Russell Atkins died
the same week as Charles Bukowski's birthday
and another poet is jacked beyond fact
to abandon everything he once thought mattered

The poems, the tours, the blurs, blurbs and blues
the repeated paying of dues, the soul eating
social media, the out-bleeding, the needy, greedy
semblance of mattering, the coarse spattering
of politics and parlor tricks, the pretense

Of glamor in overdrinking and underthinking
and waking up remorseful and shrinking
and stinking in the name of kicks and glory
and another diluted and denuded story—

Or is that deluded?—the all for one and one
two, free for all, copious alcohol, the bad speed
and weedy need for speedy and infinitely recurring
validation amid endlessly recurring frustration

And climate devastation and one nation under
a myth-god gone missing and perpetual pissing
of plastic rain and failure, toxic train derail-ure
and is it pronounced Pale a steen or Pale a stein?

What is in John's Basement?

And what about the fine, lean, stripped-bare bride,
her doom and gloom groom, the shot glass bleeding
hide and seek of war up the backside, the thirst
for slow-crawl suicide and another poet is
about to chuck
it all, say fuck it all, the brilliance, ebullience, the extra-ultra

Feckless bullshit siren's call, the Bojangles tangle
of fall and response, the once in a lifetime squandered
the ponderous wander toward go-juice, germ jam
gerbil wheel, jealous textbook squeal and Jesus

Complex—because yes, it's anything but simple
—*yet we must* pop the pimple of ego, stop revering the pus,
refuse to continue kicking our own bleeding heads and hearts
with the steel toe
of sorrow and resignation and begin, and again and forever
begin

To shimmy and shimmer and shine, warm and willing
and grin in the face of oblivion as this, our perfect
opportunity beckons: to live, not die, blazing forth
and wide and far like the solar wind we are

Commander Cornelius Anne Bigsby III

Stormy Night

By Merilee Johnson

It was a dark and stormy night. The door to John's basement slowly creaked open. In the darkness, the sound of one heavy step on the top stair … the second stair … the third. A pause. Labored breathing.

The steps resumed: fourth stair … fifth ... sixth. Another pause. More heavy breathing.

A hard rain beat against the windows. Thunder clapped, getting closer. Lightning briefly illuminated the room. A bulky figure continued slowly down the stairs. Seventh … eighth … ninth … tenth. A pause. Gasping for air.

"Oh God," a woman's voice muttered. Another step … another. Then she screamed. The sound of something weighty falling, hitting a garbage can, the lid clanging as it rolled away.

The thunder. The lightning. A fierce wind had kicked up, moaning in the basement … or was that the woman moaning?

"John!" the woman hollered hoarsely, then cleared her throat and tried again. "John!" Heavy breathing.

A man's voice at the top of the stairs. "Mom?" He tried the switch. "Oh, the light doesn't work!"

What is in John's Basement?

She grunted. "I can't see a dern thing down here, 'cep when there's lightning."

"Why are you down there?"

"Pickles. For the salad."

A lightning flash briefly illuminated John's thin figure. At the bottom of the stairs, his mother embraced an overturned garbage can.

"Oh my god! Are you OK?" he asked.

"I fell! I missed the last step or two."

"Let me get a flashlight. Be right back."

She sighed.

Shortly, a flashlight beam emanated from the top of the stairs and bounced with John's footfalls as he descended. "The lights are off upstairs now, too."

"Oh no," she said. "The food will spoil if the electricity's off much longer."

John knelt in front of her, the flashlight illuminating her figure. "We need to worry about <u>you</u> first. Do you hurt anywhere? Do you think anything's broken?"

Commander Cornelius Anne Bigsby III

Thunder crackled. Lightning flashed. The rain sounded even harder. They heard a gurgle at the drain. John shone his flashlight over and saw water seeping in through the windows.

"Mom, we've got to get you upstairs! Are you feeling well enough for that?"

"Well, I don't want to drown! If it comes to _that_ much water."

"Hopefully there won't be more than usual. The sump pump oughta kick in soon. But here, let me try and help you up." He hung the flashlight from the ceiling first.

He grunted as he tried to pull his mother into a seated position. "Oof. Can you put your arms around me?"

"No," she said, on the verge of tears.

"Well, I know how I can help you, Mom." He put on a rubber werewolf mask, then howled. "Owwwww-oooooo!"

She sighed. "Not that again."

"Well, I'm a wimp, Mom. I admit it. I need more strength to lift you up the stairs. And until we buy you a chairlift, this will have to do. Owwwwww-ooooooo!"

"John, don't bite me, though. You know it really freaks me out when you do this."

John popped his arms and legs out one by one as his werewolf form took shape. "Uh! Uh! Uh! Uh!"

John reached down for his mother. She took his hands and stood. He grabbed the flashlight and put it in his teeth. Mom stayed close to John as they ascended the stairs, one of his arms around her, one hand holding hers.

Commander Cornelius Anne Bigsby III

Shifting Shapes

By Tyler Frederick

The first step of shape-shifting
Is to exhaust all other options
Past what the seer saw
The thinker thought
The somersault of cycles
Spinning thru the cosmic constellations
forwards, onwards!

Suspend all disbelief

Disengage allegiance
to words you've been taught
to wonder in
Confront again
the urge to plunder and pillage
and ponder
The what ifs
that make you consider that
what is may not be so

The second step is just to go
Slowly, full throttle, into the stillness

The third step is...
Redacted
Even if I could tell you
You wouldn't be able to listen

The sound of metamorphosis
is not within the range
a human ear can interpret, plus

What is in John's Basement?

The final step
Is the realization that
To shape shift
All you have to do is exist

To become who you wanna be though?
Well
You gotta do that...
With intention.

Commander Cornelius Anne Bigsby III

The List

By Frogg Corpse

Three dead hookers and a laser light show.
Keith Richards cocaine collection.
(If he could keep one. . .)
Hannibal Lector's guide on binging and purging.
One Nancy Reagan blowup doll.
Two siamese sisters scissoring in a DJ booth.
Burt Bacharach's Backdoor Bonanza.
Sean Penn's Pencil.
Putin's passcode.
Tiny Tim's Fuck Hut.
Forty-four pounds of mescaline
And a new federal charge.
Two pairs of left-handed socks.
A massive mime orgy: (Quiet on the Set!) Shhh!
A condom, a plunger, and an old Fingerhut catalog.
Chris Hansen & the Bad Time Band.
The last brick & mortar store.
Your Great Aunt Esmeralda's Ball Gag.
George W. Bush painting a puppy.
Florence Henderson's Nightgown.
Bettie White covered in cum.
Every beanie baby your uncle went broke for.
Three chapter seven bankruptcies.
A crack whore, a tiki bar,
And a whole lot of cough drops.
Richard Nixon's fifth chin.
Your dead grandmother's clown collection.
Larry Craig toe-tapping.
Dick-head Dale and his Walmart buddies.

What is in John's Basement?

One colossal cock strapped to a chainsaw.
That missing tape from 8MM.
A vatican priest, and nine nuns crying.
Seven girl scouts and a restraining order.
3 Ninjas, a dump truck,
And that slurpee machine from Encino Man.
Hey, I am not a comedian,
They don't pay me to write.
But they said I could: "Wheeze the Juice!"

Commander Cornelius Anne Bigsby III

Dirge of the Vineyard

By Gary Huskisson

A dystopian soundtrack of disrepair and abandonment,
The Mother of all Katrina's curses up a storm's existence.
Each Wiley Ole Rufus must provide an offering
To be served to "The Provider" at the gallows, beyond the
wasteland.

It is dem der bones that decompose in the landfill.
There is always a debt to be repaid, a large duck walk bill   .

Such sacrifice can be a blood donation, capital, or some
financial investment.
for this transaction to achieve full satisfaction,
The Elephants Provider will only accept one's soul or salvation.
The Lord will be exalted for the righteousness,

Pronounce woe on the sinners, the mockers and the street
corner dealers

Summon, the underbelly to make peace with their maker, assess
the needs of the honorary pallbearers.
Never the bride always the pacemaker,
Wiley Ole Rufus measures his stride as their band leader.

A deadpan drum beats a hum.
A false note and a puff of black smoke—
Time for the saints to extract their pain.
Death by blues, there is never a right time for a change.
A witch's brew is always a white disdain,
Insatiable, a sweet creole marinade.

What is in John's Basement?

The Godfather is naked; James Bond has fainted
The new clothes are being worn by werewolves in sheep's
clothing.

Wiley Ole Rufus steps out to a lingering mercy chorus,
Must get to the end of the block before the sky turns blue.
Barbed wire fences fill the darkness,
Bats and ravens monitor the progress of Wiley Ole Rufus.

In the quest to get their dues,
They must stay in tune and rhyme in time to lay beside the
unmarked tomb.
The onlookers hold candles that flicker,
Each flame is ghosted by a ghost and the governors at Rikers.

As memories rise that they cherish most,
Each note a tear, each chord a plea,
For those who've passed, for what can't be—
Mardi Gras black roses are withering down Bourbon Street.

The Brass Taps squirm an opening bar that crows.
Prowling vultures are ready to pounce on strays that chew on
any leftovers.
These insurgents are the counterintelligence.
They will gleefully consume any resistance.

Sabre-toothed mongrel growling dogs wear Men in Black
glasses.
Weeping and wallowing, Minotaurs join the procession at the
intersection,
The home of gangbangers, demons, goblins, and street
mobsters.
A hollow clarinet droops a note from the passive walkers.

Commander Cornelius Anne Bigsby III

Keystone Cops masquerade in disguise, walking and talking to
the beat of their drum,

Ignoring the rapists and murderers.
While the White House is subject to another court summons,
Big Ben has eroded away from the House of Commons.

No bongs, no bings, no time, no converse, no insurrection—
just increasing polarization.

Tracking viruses and deviants, every movement, every sound is
recorded on closed-circuit television,
Watching the cats and dogs being eaten by Ohio residents.
Into the wasteland—isolation, loneliness, a picture of
desolation.

The wind moans in grief and the rainstorm billows in vain;
The trees are barren and their branches strain.
It is imperative that Wiley Ole Rufus stay in their lane.
The shadows are discreet, silence weeps,
A dirge unfolds, the heart it keeps,

With whispered sighs and mournful tones,
It echoes through the relics of unforeseen milestones.
A frog sparrow croaks, once bright and bold,
Now sings of tales that time has told,
Of fleeting joys and dreams now lost,
In the chill of dusk, they count the cost.

The fiber optics under the pavement cracks are consumed
                         with misogyny and structural racism.

What is in John's Basement?

It is a long trek to the bottom rung of the ladder.
Cobras and adders disperse their constriction, anticipating some
hide or fodder.

Starting with cymbals and with Ole Wiley's high hat, all the
percussion, including the ethnic electronic triangle, is rampaged
by the lack of prohibition.

The failing cable providers are part of the conspiracy.
They make a daily pilgrimage to every structure systematically—
Criminal justice, health, wealth, housing, and education.
Decay, despair, and poverty complete the toxic fusion.
Wiley Ole Rufus frets as the guitar string plucks, dissolving into
micros.
A sharp intake of breath from the polished sousaphone,
Followed by a deep exhale from Wiley Ole Rufus's trombone.
"Piccolo, oh piccolo, summon a legion of zombies," all the way
to the gallows."
Wiley Ole Rufus's clarinet whistles in the hollow,
Trolled by a venomous oboe. Vultures gather all the sorrow;
They carry forth the names to be mourned.
In every joyous anthem, a rebirth is found.
Let the Vineyard Dirge weave through the night,

A tapestry of loss and light,
For in the sorrow, we find grace;
In every ending, a new embrace.
This dystopian dirge on any earth
Is how human sin and rejection are dealt
By God's love and grace.
Their band marching steps follow no shadows;

Commander Cornelius Anne Bigsby III

Dreams are left to wither, hindered by barricades of suspicion.
The fiber optics under the pavement cracks are consumed with
structural racism.
It is a long trek to the bottom rung of the gallows.
The failing cable providers are part of the conspiracy.
They make a daily pilgrimage to every structure systematically—
Criminal justice, health, wealth, housing, and education.
Decay, despair, and poverty complete the toxic fusion.

The white fluffy clouds are black,
Full of torment, waffle, and blunder.
Whispers and tales are bluster,
Echoes of a turbulent regime.
Battens and truncheons rattle railings and chains,
Sandwich boards hollow in the halls of justice, where the scales
bear the stain.
While the black felines and the crazy jazz cats have escaped out
of the drains

The street cleaners and the refuse collectors are fed on
Machiavellian grain

Repent your sins and follow the saints; the best prediction is a
slow death conviction.
The real bandleader reside at house of disrepute called The
Draconian
The scaffolding for the Newspeak foundations is built on
indigenous land,

What is in John's Basement?

Where some rise and some fall.
Invisible barriers stand, a fortress for them all.
They always have a cigar-smoking benefactor to call.
Rejuvenation's golden promise is a door that's often locked,
While Tena pants slither, skid-marked toilets are blocked.
In spite of insidious capitalist finger clicks,
On X the canaries still tweet
The air is toxic, with silence, and the truth is hard to find.
Housing dreams deferred in neighborhoods confined,
Health and wealth are tangled in a web of deep despair.
On golden pathways, the privileged walk, oblivious, ignorant,
and unaware.
The local snakes constrict the underbelly into their lair.

A system rigged and twisted,
Where opportunity's a game.
The players roll weighted dice;
The stakes are never the same.
Who cares about the fate of Miss Adelaide?
The Specials menu is Spam and Strife
Innate voices rise like thunder,
Diminishing the value of life.
Time for the walls at the end of the block to be torn.
The sight of the gallows makes one quake;
For every heart that's heavy, there's a spirit that won't break.

The fiber optics must "enlarge the place of their tent, stretch
their curtains wide, not holding back, and lengthen their cords
and strengthen their stakes." (Isaiah 54:2 NIV)
It is time once again for The Song of the Vineyard to sing.
Time for good to be classed as evil,

Commander Cornelius Anne Bigsby III

As the blue flame ignites a light for darkness,
A shovel of sweet lemons to replace the taste of bitter. (Isaiah 5
NIV)
The Lord will be exalted for righteousness,
He will summon the nations to judge his people.
With the passing of Wiley Ole Rufus, the love for the vineyard
experiences a metamorphic transformation into a splintered
section of the bespoke gallows.

At the end of the block, there is only one thing to find:
That Wiley Ole Rufus has left his swag bag behind with ACME
dynamite
For the sake of mankind.
The world doesn't care about morals
'Cause as the world is insane,
And Wiley Ole Rufus does not feel any sorrow,
And it is just The Blues to blame.
"No more silent suffering, no more shadows cast,
An amnesty for all the brass,
To forge bridges that will last."
Now the saints can go marching in;
(The Song of the Vineyard)
They dug it up and cleared it of stones and planted it with the
choicest vines.
The remains of Wiley Ole Rufus built a watchtower in it and
cut out a winepress as well.
They looked for a crop of good grapes, but it yielded only bad
fruit.
"Now you dwellers in Jerusalem and people of Judah, judge
between me and my vineyard."
(Isaiah 5:2-4)
Oh, when the saints go marching,
They are going to be in that Vineyard
When the saints go marching in.

What is in John's Basement?

The Real Dream The Real Inquisition

By Eddy Foreman

"I am doing the best I can
I am telling you the truth Officer Dan!
Am I in trouble here?"

My neighbor's name is John.
Is he a strange guy?
I suspected him from the start.
      When I say hello, says "good-bye."
     I ask him, "How is it going?

      But he responds, "Why?".
When I see him, I always sigh.
He is a wet blanket.

The neighborhood was nothing special.
 Everyone kept to themselves.
 Everyone behaved either simply or civilly.
 The neighborhood motto was everyone stay mindful of
strangers and yourselves.

"At the time I was thinking…"

Call the cops, I could.
But do I want all that attention and publicity?
 No!
I need to protect this great neighborhood.
All that noise and flashing lights remind me of the city.
No one needs that.

If I could find out what happened.
I could send the police some evidence, which would do some
good.

      Commander Cornelius Anne Bigsby III

Be good for me.

"This is what I saw, see"

I moved into this neighborhood for tranquility.
I hated the hustle and bustle of the city.
 I want a life with more peaceful serenity.
With all that city noise, I wouldn't live past fifty.

This neighborhood reminds me of a town.
Where everyone knows each other like a sister, like a brother.
I think this is the best neighborhood around.
We all adore
And appreciate the neighbors.

I remembered that he moved here a while ago.
He made a ton of food to eat for us at their housewarming.
All of it gluten-free, without barley, rye, or wheat.
The taste made you move your hands and feet.
The sandwiches were good, and the wine was sweet.
It was John and his wife.
He was more happy than shallow.
She was the sun in his life.
John had a huge smile on his face.
Nothing in his house was out of place.
He never leaves anything to waste.
He always carries an expensive attaché case.
He had a welcome party at his house.
It was so clean; you wouldn't see a mouse.
There were a ton of pictures of Jimbo er John and his spouse.
He always wore charcoal suits, while his wife wore a perfectly
pressed satin blouse.
Everything was so perfect, too perfect.
It was odd.

What is in John's Basement?

  I asked others, "What's with John?"
They didn't answer and didn't go on.
 The conversation was brief but not long.
 I wonder what in the world did I stumble upon?

One of my ideas is: Can John er, Jimbo be a killer?
He was overly happy and nice, and friendly.
His presence did make the air feel a bit thinner.
But now, he is beginning to act odd, strange, and differently.

John told me about his wife dying from cancer.
I didn't see his wife after that.
Jimbo er John did not seem himself.
John didn't look right.
He was quite a sight.
I wanted to ask but didn't.
 I remained calm and quiet, which took all my might.

I pondered; He didn't let me go into his locked room.
My curiosity started to bloom.
My ideas came like a raging monsoon.
Will it be a revelation or my doom?

Scheming at this point
To find out if John is a killer
What is in the basement?
I grabbed my ski mask, a pick lock, and a flashlight.

I know, it didn't feel right.
I quickly sneaked out of everyone's sight.
I was as a ghostly shadow in the night.

I was walking around till I saw the basement door.
  I reached, then I heard, "why are doing that for?"
 It shakes my hearty core.

Commander Cornelius Anne Bigsby III

A voice asked, "Do you want somewhere else to explore?"

"The next thing I know I am out like a light conked in the head with a rubber chicken. when I woke up."

This is so crazy, weird, and unfair.
 I heard his squeaks, honks, and kazoo sounds.
I was bound in a wooden chair.
I had only my mask and underwear.
I was stuck in a mask and in my underwear.
 I'm being tormented by a demented clown.
The unknown voice said, "Sorry about your clothes; you look a bit stuffy."
I screamed, "Why did you take my clothes?"
The unknown voice said, "You were beginning to look like my cat, Fluffy."
I said, "I felt dirty, embarrassed, and exposed."

The room was colorful, like a circus. it felt like I was the main attraction.
 I felt terrified, scared, and a bit nervous.
My mind couldn't boggle these unique and vivid distractions.

I saw a pale face with a big red nose.
He slowly put my face to his rose.
 Squirt!
Water arose.

He said you want some answers, I suppose.

The stranger said, "Well, stranger. Welcome to my basement.
My name is Jimbo the clown.
I hope to fill you full of childish amazement.
Welcome to clowning around!"

What is in John's Basement?

He started telling me jokes.
 He started to act them out.
Jimbo said, "Why shouldn't you date a blow-up doll? because it's full of hot air."
My fear started to fall. Jimbo said, "I have plenty of jokes to share."

       Jimbo er, John asked, "Why I should not nap in a banana hammock?"
       I said, "Why?" John er, Jimbo replied, "People don't
       find it appealing…   get it they are afraid they will slip.!"
I was laughing and surprised. This joke made me crazy, and drool dripped right over my lower lip.
Jimbo unties me. I gave him a big hug.
       He said, "Sor...."
       But I disagree and interrupt.
       I said, "Dirt under the rug."
Jimbo took off my mask. Jimbo had sadness on his face.
       I yelled, "I had a blast!"
 Jimbo stumbled to find his place.

And on a wooden chair next to me he sat.
And tears ruined his clown make up.
And he softly said," we moved here because she was sick."
       "I started clowning to help her feel better."
       "We knew this was a good place."
       "with good doctors and such"
       "I wished we had more time"
She always thought he was funny.
It's what he did to romance her.
 It always made her sunny.
       Jimbo er, John said, "You can stay as long as you like."
       I said, "This was weird. What an experience!"
       Jimbo er, John said, "You and I are so much alike."
       I said, "No! Really! You serious!"

Commander Cornelius Anne Bigsby III

Jimbo opened his house's backdoor to let me out.
 I quickly sneaked out and rushed out.
	Jimbo said, "I HOPE YOU GOT WHAT YOU CAME FOR!" Ha ha.
	I said, "Shhhhhhhhhhhh! There's no need to shout."

"Is this where you want me to sign this statement ?"

What is in John's Basement?

What?

By Jonathan S. Baker

Welp,
doctor says
it's bowel cancer.

Commander Cornelius Anne Bigsby III

Why I Am Not a Horror Movie Clown

By Darrell Parry

First off,
I'm really bad at balloon animals.
I get the concept but… I don't know.
I think I'm always afraid
I'm going to pop them before I'm finished.
That makes me a little squeamish
and too timid to twist them properly.

Clowning requires a lot
of these very specialized skills
and I hear that clown college
is as bad as boot camp
and that the big 3 only accept
something like 50 applicants per year.

It sounds stressful.

Sure, there are thousands of
amateur part-time clowns.
That would be an easier option,
but who wants to be
a part-time, amateur horror movie clown?
How does that look on a resume?
What kind of workplace would hire me?

What is in John's Basement?

Workplace is an important factor.
Evil clowns are always relegated
to carnivals and birthday parties
or, most often, circuses.
 Yet I have never seen a killer clown
interacting with elephants.
I don't see the point of having a circus motif
to your murder spree if you're not even
going to get to play with elephants.

And the quality of the victims?
They're just like every other horror movie slasher:
high teen-agers parking with their latest chick
or partying in their friend's basement,
except that with clowns you have to add
whiny children into the mix.

Clowns never even get to stalk
the badly behaved kids at restaurants,
the playground bullies,
or the parents that raise those types of kids.
That might at least provide
some character motivation
and give the audience something to root for.

Commander Cornelius Anne Bigsby III

But we're talking horror movies here
and I guess you're not supposed
to root for the clown.
The point is for everyone to
to look at the victims and think
"That could be me,"
or "That could be my kid.,"
and chances are that you and your kids
would be pretty boring
and pointless murder victims.

That's probably a good thing for you
in real life, but kinda sucks
for all the poor horror movie
murder clowns out there,
stuck in their never-ending cycle
of tired slasher cliches
filled with gratuitous unrealistic gore,
Pulling
Ripping
Squeezing
Slicing bodies
waiting for them to pop
like balloon animals.
(Which we have already established
that I'm bad at because of the popping part.)

What is in John's Basement?

Now that I think about it
I'd probably be pretty squeamish
about the murder part too.
I'm somewhat neurotic about messes
I'd be okay with the blood, I think,
I just wouldn't want it all over the place.

I can barely take all the spilled beer
and pretzel crumbs on the floor.
I don't know,
Maybe I should stop daydreaming,
get out of this corner,
grab a drink,
get a little paper hat
and join the party.

I'd get myself a slice of cake, too,
but suddenly I don't feel like
going anywhere near the knife

Commander Cornelius Anne Bigsby III

BUSTED

By Clive Oseman

I never meant anyone any harm. I needed money and I found a market waiting to be explored. Now I'm about to be exposed and I guess I must face up to the fact that my actions have left a trail of innocent victims in their wake. I would say I'm sorry, but I'm only sorry I have been found out. I don't give a shit about other people and don't do false apologies. I care only for myself and the fact that not only will my source of income dry up, but I could end up in jail.

I don't believe in paying blackmailers. That's a mug's game. A never-ending cycle of fear and expense, so screw it. I'm going to reveal all, before my ex does. I'm ready to face the consequences.

I got the idea when I was staying in a hostel many years ago. I had a gambling problem. I needed the money. I considered killing people and selling their organs, but as I faint at the sight of blood and had no idea who I could sell them to (and didn't have a fridge or freezer) it was a non-starter. Then I had a eureka moment. Toenails. I would wait until everyone was asleep and would very carefully take a clipping of people's toenails.

What is in John's Basement?

Who knew? There is a large market for celebrity toenail clippings! So, I would take a clipping from some random in the dorm and sell it as David Beckham's, or Tom Cruise's, or whatever the customer wanted. It's incredible the prices people will pay if the clippings are supplied with a forged certificate of authenticity. I could even afford to pay the nobodies for their nails, but why pay when collecting the free samples gives such a rush? The smell of cheese has always turned me on. Oh yes! The big toe is the most lucrative, which turns logic on its head because they are always the easiest to collect.

What? Yes, of course I used chloroform on the suppliers. I'm not stupid.

Anyway, I'm starting to sound a little creepy now, so this is it, my confession in full. The museum I was planning on opening in Vladivostok (the most lucrative market by a considerable distance) will not be happening. All because I committed adultery with the woman supplying the certificates. I didn't even ask her for a clipping, but my wife took umbrage when she found out. She expected clippings from everyone I slept with. That was the agreement. I broke the rules. She divorced me and is now blackmailing me. I'm trapped. She knows where I store them and will say she just thought I had a fetish. Now she wants a genuine clipping from Prince Harry, complete with a video of me taking it, which would fetch about 750k, or she will go to the cops. I'm ruined. I could probably get Andrew, but she said no to that. She couldn't give it away.
Crazy, but true

Commander Cornelius Anne Bigsby III

Rune

By K.R. Morrison

I cast nine switchblades

made of my skin, black cactus
reminders I bury in you

I resurrect in memory basements

my naked ghost dances
ice cold footprints

through your backbone
mazes. I kick rocks

turn over stones, I graffiti soul
ruins so those Conquistadoras

smell our magick
so your wounds know

I cast nine gritas

in you, bruja echoes
for every poema that holds you

like my bed, for every meal
you eat alone

that tastes of me
so every painting

What is in John's Basement?

or story made by left hands
summon you and me

for new moons that turn
her back from your hands

I cast your nights dark

as the dead end you left
          in a sweet witch's heart

Commander Cornelius Anne Bigsby III

The Heat

By *Michael Sindler*

You can escape the sun.
The blue shade of the pine forest
screens the worst of the glare,
filtering the pale
yellow incandescence.
Your sweat-soaked sleeves,
buttoned at wrists—
tightly woven straw hat
glued to dank locks—
britches clinging to thighs—
weighing you down with perspiration—
prove that humidity, on the other hand,
is inescapable—unrelenting.
In a drier clime, this might be bearable,
but in this lonely wood
outside this small southern town,
it's torture.
Your tongue swollen,
mouth and throat dry as the cracking
pinestraw you trample on.
You feel nearly defeated,
ready to lie down under a tree and let
sleep overtake you—slowly braising—
stewing in the sopping heat.
But you will not allow yourself
to become the sacrificial lamb
resting before carving,
so you stumble and stride on
in search of safety.

What is in John's Basement?

You can't hear any sounds
other than natural ones carried
on the slight breeze
breaking the stagnant humidity.
Bird calls, pinecones and branches falling,
nothing else.
But you know sounds will come.
Heavy feet, running in thick boots.
Sounds of whooping.
Your name being called
as a taunt and threat.
This is the real heat.
The heat of fear.
You must keep moving,
because they will be coming.
If only you could run.

Commander Cornelius Anne Bigsby III

Laughing-Out, Life
By LKN

my head, latched
cracking the bones
into a second hand giveaway
a free pass to lash life at 3.02am

i could see time—break
a filament of pain, now slid open
under the carpet
soaked of my shadow

there's a guffaw in my shut jaw
gagging on the echoes, muttering
i told you... i'll bleed you
as the manic joke fills the room

and my name is the punchline
my body twitched
betwixt on a clacking cackling
splattering in my hollow body

my insides, emptied by snicker
why is there a smirk on my wrist
twisted, sniggering
i told you... i'll get you
the sinister is real

What is in John's Basement?

silent screams, rang into loud whispers
the panting on the waking evening
was the nightmare dreaming
as i reached for the lamp on my left

there's a knife, besides the clock
2.58am pointed to the mirror

why am i smiling?!!

Commander Cornelius Anne Bigsby III

Depth Charge

By Fin Hall

Hello below, The secret is out.
Outwith the realms of your inner thoughts. Crumbling echoes
Search out deep past memories
Recalling things you never thought you knew.
The whisper of a rumour Clawing , gnawing,
Drawing back the blinds
Of drunken poems Sunken in the beneath,
Where fear has maybe blinded you,
And the darkness,
Bitter darkness,
Trembling and foregoing,
Weeps as truth escapes.
Like an unbroken stallion,
Set free in the black forest
Of an unknown land,
Unafraid and hopeful,
Waiting for the morning light.
Sullen and grey,
But still,
Still, and with a hint of glimmer,
Ready to reveal.
As wisps of hope,
Like smoke from incense sticks
Of unfamiliar scents,
Ascend to vanish
In the nothingness
 Of the future
Where your truths shall be revealed.
If only you permit.

What is in John's Basement?

Empty bed

By Jon Wesick

Dara is lying on her back beside me when I open my eyes. Wearing only cotton panties decorated with tiny, printed flowers, she's within my reach. Skin the amber of maple syrup, stomach flat, nipples brown, legs hinting at the muscle beneath, and breasts' graceful curves of tension resisting gravity. Her presence in my bed is rare as finding a platinum coin on the sidewalk. Only her touch can smooth life's jagged edges from my flesh that stings from broken glass and rusty barbed wire. I worry she's not tough enough. How good it would feel to pull her body into mine. I reach

and I'm staring at a bookcase of dictionaries and writing manuals from a bed that's been empty for over a decade. The twilight glow from a laptop, showing videos that help me sleep, illuminates my room. A guy in a black suit and skinny tie interviews a professor with a bald crown, named Tungsten. He wears wire-rimmed glasses and a tan sweater under his blue blazer. Instead of describing the universe with mathematics, he wants to simulate it via simple algorithms at the subatomic scale, called cellular automata.

I load the washing machine sitting atop the cracked linoleum in her parents' basement. Dara lies on a couch in the den. The TV's on but I don't pay attention.
"Where do you want to go on vacation?" I sit next to her.
We have two weeks to drive somewhere on the East Coast. New York City is the obvious choice.
"Ever been to Atlanta?" I lean forward and kiss her belly through a gap the missing button left on her soft, plaid shirt.
Her flesh is soothing as a warm bath against my lips. I give myself over to her pleasure but somehow in this netherworld of dreams, she returns the favor.

Commander Cornelius Anne Bigsby III

Still old, still fat, still unlikely to find a lover I can tolerate, I wake alone in my bed. I don't like the stranger I see in the mirror with bags under hound-dog eyes and a bald spot shaped like Eurasia with tufts of crabgrass in Berlin and Vladivostok. It's a tired cliché, one I never thought I'd become. On my laptop, the professor says his simulation can reproduce Einstein's theory of gravity.

"Instead of using the computer's master clock, each thread has its own timepiece," he continues.

That's just relativity. Einstein said time moves at different rates depending on the observer. I close my eyes and listen.

"Are you even real?" I ask Dara. "Every time I hold you, I end up with an armful of mist."
"I'm real."
I kiss her lips. Her body is warm and firm but yields just the right amount against my chest.

Alone again. There's a cuneiform tablet on my laptop's screen as a voice recites the *Enuma Elish*, the Babylonian creation epic. Here, the primordial waters of Apsu and Tiamat mingled to give birth to the gods. Sometime after Marduk defeats chaos, I roll over and fall into a dreamless sleep.

How To Revive
By Sophia Falco

Big Bad Wolf, the band, burped up their playlist of songs. Rocking out in the tiny wine bar equipped with their repertoire of music; the previous generation as I was sitting outside on a wooden chair next to a local shop. Unlike the others, I wasn't thinking about the time of night the rain was supposed to roll in.

One older lady, probably high, in a black dress with a push-up bra walked up to me unsteadily with her head titled to the right bluntly questioned me:
"Are you happy or sad?"
I replied: "Do you want the real answer?"
After our short conversation, she walked away still dazed yet satisfied but still somehow unsatisfied leaving me by myself.

I started staring hard at the red fabric overhead, those dangling lights that were not all aligned properly still sitting outside of their outside seating area. I was hoping to become dissociated; half listening to the blaring blurring music until one song drew me in. "Have You Ever Seen The Rain" by Creedance Clearwater Revival.

One dancer outstretched his arms, but body still on the dance floor signaled to whom; I'm not sure, that the rain had come as a few heavy drops fell like a conglomeration of teardrops. He pretended to catch them.

Commander Cornelius Anne Bigsby III

I peeked in. I couldn't see my father, but guessing he was still dancing and grooving to that song. Whereas this took me back a decade ago when we were simply sitting in his parked car. He asked, me with all the seriousness that is not typically seen; his eyes glazed with tears, when that same song played; "What do these lyrics mean? Because they make me sad." (That sadness struck a cord in me, too.)

Now, I wondered, in the moment of dancing fever if the lyrics still struck his heart strings of sorrow, certainly those words struck mine knowingly this past history. Perhaps this still does. Maybe only certain type of poets or let's break it down further—maybe only certain type of people know the answer or maybe only certain humans are moved by this music to point of the feeling of sadness.

The rain comin' down on a sunny day was like angels—not giving dust, but instead a hit of sorrow ((kinetic energy)) running through blue veins as reality seems too joyous as the light is strong, warm, as drunk people are laughing and unprepared for the weather. They're wearing sandals not giving a shit if their feet get wet, the answer might lie in the sky. Why? Well that is between him and I.

What is in John's Basement?

Weight of Absence (a Runway of Lost Chances)

By Phynne~Belle

The suspended glass window shelf lined up with the wide expanse of blue-black pavement bordering the bobbing waves of the Pacific Ocean just beyond it. It had become a runway for the six pairs of cheerful, buttercup crochet booties placed in a neat row like tiny, severed feet. A runway of happy, buoyant crafts in perpetual standby, waiting to go nowhere. They reminded me in that moment, of an isolated childhood memory— watching planes lift off and return from the seemingly endless strip of tarmac at Miramar Naval Air Station on a late summer day.

I marvel at how I sustain this memory above others, my subconscious holding it up to the light to break apart and prism, creating its own realities, each one fracturing and telling its own story. Not all the stories stay to bask in daylight. Not all the planes are guided safely back. Not all the unnamed children will be present to blow out the candles on their first birthday. Some stories know better than to trust a failing memory, an unreliable narrator— they will choose the feeble death— in stop and go flashes of recognition, agony drawn out, a feigned struggle to remain among the living, to be remembered. They are the wound choosing to festers until they summon the grace to bleed out.

My mind floods with uncertainty— did this truly happen, the way I revisit it in my mind, joyful, boundless, carefree? I am terrified as realization dawns, how my mind will attempt to buffer my pain and cushion me in illusion, picking up scraps of idyllic moments at will, and piecing together a story to let float to the surface.

Commander Cornelius Anne Bigsby III

My mind, my existence, a fine-wrought patchwork of borrowed and fabricated mental photographs. I am the mad doctor's creature. I am a monster with a discordant body of recollections. I stitched the picture of this life together with my own compassionate deceit.

In this waking dream I now wander through an ever-changing scenario, walking from room to room, from house to house, treading a linear ribbon, an onyx void, its steady, bright yellow line leading me infinitely.

A dream dictates unspoken rules: you must never know what you seek, or question what you hope to find.

The booties reappear in sharp focus before my eyes— I fight to raise them to the surface of the placid blue sky and remember to whom they belong.

Where have the babies gone?

Is each pair of shoes, a child of mine
lost
mourned
dreamed about?

Inside my womb I furnished its vacant space with a phantom cradle and carriage.

An infant blinks, confused, against the unfamiliar sunlight that burns through her fragile eyelids.

An empty womb is a haunted house where ghosts can echo their forgotten lullabies.

An infant emits a lusty cry, shrieks at the first sensation of oxygen inflating her tiny lungs.

What is in John's Basement?

*I failed her
for she does
not know
she is dead.*

The booties stand still in the foreground, waiting. Their jaunty, sunshine color have become a cruel joke, a mockery of my grief.

Beyond them, the fighter jets appear one by one out of thin air between the sultry heat and picture-perfect clouds that have decided to hover over the barren taxiway. They come in for a flawless landing, consume the full length of the wavering pitch black concrete before lifting off to depart, weightless. This pattern they do in an unceasing loop— they, too, seek answers that will not arrive. The roar in their engines as they leave me is a cacophony like despair. It is a moving picture, the twisted, heartbreaking beauty of it all, taunting my sanity.

Commander Cornelius Anne Bigsby III

Cliff Notes for Living on the Edge

By Tyler Frederick

John keeps his secrets in the basement, in the fall out shelter.
How else could he keep
the helter skelter to himself?

He don't let nobody down there. The door handle, hidden in
the bookshelf. The books, all banned. But no one is coming to
save him, no one can.

That's how he likes it.

Just leave him with his plastic bags full of plastic bags and all
the cans, crushed.
Bottles, some broken. Glass - yeah,
watch for the broken glass. Little window shattered past March
- hasn't gotten it fixed.

The spiderwebs keep the bugs out - he puts every spider he
finds in that windowsill. Let's 'em duke it out, next to the box
of broken promises, and one of forgotten dreams.

What is in John's Basement?

A filing cabinet full of false hopes and wasn't what it seemeds.
And oh wells and ah ha's.
Should've beens and never was.
Should've known and never does.
Some too lates, some too soons.
A couple maybe next times...
But not in this lifetime,
Sucker.

John keeps the fall out locked up.
It's his shelter.
Nobody's gonna save him.

Commander Cornelius Anne Bigsby III

Fearful Hope Lingers

By hil hoover

but where is your joy?
did you hide it beneath the floor
where no one could crush it
did you take it out back and
finish the job when it began to
falter
(with the gun your father gave you
on some childhood birthday -
too young, too soon, too innocent
for this responsibility)
or did you
(like so many of us)
hide it away in boxes and
store it in some basement corner
in hopes of preserving the pieces
to be rifled through on a future date?

because to be untouchable to the world
is the only way to keep such a thing.

is that why you are afraid to open the door?

your pretense of celebration on some significant date
faltering with each step as you
consider retrieving some decoration or
last-minute libation

What is in John's Basement?

because if you look,
you'll know for sure
if any scrap of genuine
feeling is left
crouching in some cobweb-corner

easier to imagine
you fear the ghost
of some previous resident
or a demon summoned up
by mistake

than the nothing
that might greet you
in the dark

Commander Cornelius Anne Bigsby III

The Sorrowful Shales of Silver Creek

By Frogg Corpse

Autumn arrives as Summer recedes
Breaking the sorrowful shales of Silver Creek
Struck by a stamper that advanced in its weeds
Over dead slate mowed by the brush of two feet

A prospect of whom, is not what one needs
When the fluttering on husk lends watch on a dying thing.

A liminal breeze catching fibrous neck
Disillusion smiled
While wooden steps turned wet

Effluvium linen, segueing slumber
The lilting Ohio branches
Swaddle a night-breaths final shudder

Ebon fingers—entwined in the oak
An auger opts conjuration
Where the roots take hold.

Pick your poison... Datura or glove?

Consume for a dream—an Elysian scene,
Evermore pressed, by a timeless touch.

What is in John's Basement?

By and by, this gloom shall spread
Over the marshes and the groves,
A nightly fixture of pastures drenched
In the follie ov the wooded row,

Blessings be by the pressings seen
Lifting against a statement
Add another for thy brother
Refusing to submit an assertion as evidence.

For wicks to sing a last chirping plea
Stretching along the berm
A vigil light for evening sights
Of a witch hung by the foot.

Commander Cornelius Anne Bigsby III

Don't worry, dear boy. Have no fear.

By Ron Whitehead

Edgar Allan Poe's "The Raven" was published
January 29th, 1845, in the Evening Mirror.

He was paid 9 dollars. Poe's last words were,
"Lord, help my poor soul."

Is every thought, word, and action etched forever
in a cloud? I love to travel. Often as not

I go alone, wandering off to faraway lands,
my solo footprints on drifting sands,

walking down dusty roads,
fields of chirping crickets,

ponds of singing toads.
When I was a boy in the Kentucky wilderness,

on a cold, dark, and dreary January day,
Daddy said, "Watch this." And he shot a crow.

It fell from the sky and landed at my feet.
I held the wounded crow in my hands.

It died screaming, "Help, Help, Help!"
as a murder circled not far above our heads.

After the orange sunset, early night,
the same day, I heard soft music,

a forlorn song, coming from an old piano,
way over yonder, on a hill far away.

J.R.R. Tolkien wrote,
"I know why you seek solitude. You suffer;

What is in John's Basement?

I see it day by day. You sure you do not suffer
needlessly? There are other ways, Frodo,

other paths that we might take."
Clouds drift under the full moon, the starlit sky.

Comes a train, heading south,
whistle blowing long and low.

After it passes I stand for a while
on the warm tracks all aglow.

I find myself under the stars,
floating in a cloud, under the moon.

When I cried that night, the crow
she came to me, and rested her head

on my left shoulder. And she's been with me
all these years. She often soars away

and is gone for days. But when she returns
she brings a poem and whispers, "A gift.

I am with you. I will guide you.
Don't worry, dear boy. Have no fear."

Commander Cornelius Anne Bigsby III

Epilogue

Hunched over the dais and with a dry whiskey whisper, Commander Cornelius Anne Bigsby III speaks.

"There is honor in this horror and carnage. I stand here before you and look you square in the eyes and say not one drop of blood was wasted. Many have sacrificed and given the full measure of the offering of their humanity. We still breathe freely because of them and owe the fallen everything for their precious gift. The cost to many will never be fully appreciated. And all in the pitch of this battle are owed all we can muster.

"Today, I ask you to join this effort.

"I know those who are guarding Earth have not heard the full story. I am not one to engage in the idle telling of tall tales and the pointless war stories of old men."

Halting and near collapse, Bigsby falls silent, taking in the fullness of the present situation. Red-faced and sweating, his forehead vein bulging and fists crashing on the dais, thunder and lightning issue from the podium.

Bigsby continues, "It was near the event horizon proximal to JADES-GS-z14-0 that, that, that, all the crew of La Concepción were lost, along with the ship which was ripped plank by bolt into powdered termite dust and lost to battle, but never to our hearts and minds. I ask now for a moment of silence."

After an appropriate time has passed the Commander continues, "Today we will honor those surviving veterans of this battle of The Great Space Worm Invasion by speaking their names.

"John Angell Grant, K.R. Morrison, Dane Ince, Ron Whitehead, Bryan Franco, Deborah C. Segal, Mbonisi Zikhali Zomkhonto, Mark States, Jeff Cottrill, Michael Sindler, Antoinette Vella Payne, Jonathan S. Baker, Chiina Bloodmire, John Burroughs, Merilee Johnson, Tyler Frederick, Frogg Corpse, Gary Huskisson, Eddy Foreman, Darrell Parry, Clive Oseman, LKN, Fin Hall, Jon Wesick, Sophia Falco, Phynne~Belle, hil hoover.

"The names of these freedom fighters will linger always on the lips of those they have fought to keep safe and free. They are heroes, and after some well-deserved rest they will once more step into the arena of mayhem and destruction to defend us all.

"Enduring hope, enduring hope, is the backbone of humanity's…"

The Commander makes unintelligible grunts, punching skyward with each groan, then falls meteorlike to the floor and bursts into flames as the soft red rain falls. All are now silent.

About the Authors

John Angell Grant, wealthy retiree inventor of the sneeze guard, donates brain while still living! "It doesn't hurt if you don't think about it." Author of *The Green Notebook* ISBN13: 9798987025963

K.R. Morrison, trap door manufacturer since 1918, indicted for use of mango springs. Author of *Cauldrons* ISBN13: 9780615868745

Dane Ince, former champion eater, has hot dog title revoked for using cow stomach implant. Author of *Destiny Murder!* ISBN13: 9798987025987

Ron Whitehead, charged with feeding marshmallows to the lions, dismissed from circus job. Author of *Tapping My Own Phone* ISBN13: 978-1957654102

Bryan Franco, banned for life from domestic air travel on Proxima Centauri for offensive garlic farts. Author of *Everything I Think Is All In My Mind* ISBN13: 9781737816225

Deborah C. Segal, world record holder for sleep driving, sells entire trophy collection for a Black Hole Donut Shop franchise. Author of *In the Time of the Cloud* ISBN-13: 979-8332109171

Mbonisi Zikhali Zomkhonto, suspected international spy accused of sending coded messages in his poems, living undercover as a spoken word artist and storyteller from Africa, residing in Canada.

Mark States, by day a mild-mannered bookkeeper, by night a creped crusader of the poetry Zoomisphere. Author of *Tongue Control (The Laguna Poets Series #215* published by The Inevitable Press in 2001)

Jeff Cottrill, inventor of Instant Poutine's new flavour, Maple Syrup and Ketchup Swirl, admits adulterating the product with eel toes. Author of *Hate Story: A satirical mystery novel* ISBN13: 9780645484090

Michael Sindler, proud vegan living on a diet of gravel and razor blades, best known for his distinctively harsh voice and sharp social commentary.

Antoinette Vella Payne, criminal mastermind trafficking in mescaline sourdough starter. Author of *That's What Happens When You Live on Haight Street* ISBN13: 979-8989417209

Jonathan S. Baker, scandalizes Midwest as poet and editor at Pure Sleeze Press, apprehended skinny dipping in the Ohio River. Author of *Centaur* with co-author Tony Brewer ISBN13: 9798885964173

Chiina Bloodmire, world class dolphin racer, cleared in blood doping scandal. Author of *The Book Of Kuu* ISBN13: 979-8332439544

John Burroughs, sails spry / soul serenades, slings songshouts / skyward, sleeps seldom. Author of *The Wrest of the Worthwhile: Unselected, Uncollected and New Poems, 1983-2023* ISBN13: 979-8885969918

Merilee Johnson, retired manicurist for Trombone Fingers Willie, rumored to be mobbed up and recently released from prison after serving a hitch for Agroalgobot fraud, remains at large and dangerous.

Tyler Frederick, poet, caver, chef and fungi enthusiast, Adjutant Chef to Commander Cornelius Anne Bigsby III.

Frogg Corpse, arrested by border agents for smuggling a minivan full of dead frogs into Taiwan from Cuba, Author of *Poetry to Die By* ISBN-13: 979-8892171571

Gary Huskisson, spoken word artist and reference librarian of Alexandria, heralded as the translator of the Dead Sea Scrolls into Russianeselish.

Eddy Foreman, beloved DC stand-up comic routinely on the circuit between HD1 and Gnz11, sources indicate he and chanteuse Chimera Queen are a hot item as seen in photos of the couple on vacation on the moon of Callisto.

Darrell Parry, Muppet maker and organizer of the "make it weird, 2024" campaign, moonlights as the editor of Stick Figure Poetry Quarterly. Author of *Twists: Gathered Ephemera* ISBN13: 978-1957863047

Clive Oseman, multi-slam winning spoken word artist, widely suspected to be the ghost writer behind the international best-sellers *The Badger Only Screams On Wednesdays* and *It Flew In From The West On A Magic Cornflake*. Author of *It Could be Verse?* ISBN13: 9781913195090

LKN, Lakan is wanted in thirteen countries for penguin abuse, allegedly shown bludgeoning them with a pool noodle in viral social media video. Author of *When Stars Are Traitors* ISBN-13: 978-1739288181

Fin Hall, found guilty by a jury of his peers on six counts of putting the bop in the bop shoo bop shoo bop, Author of *Over 1800 years In the making* ISBN13: 9781304304964

Jon Wesick, professional lizard softball coach, barred for life from the Galactic League's Hall of Fame for racketeering and sports betting. Author of *The Alchemist's Grandson Changes His Name* ISBN13: 9798373511810

Sophia Falco, denies rampant rumors of being the Babushka Lady on the Grassy Knoll and is Cooper's favorite conga player according to licensing bureau records. Author of *If My Hands Were Birds: A Poem* published by UnCollected Press ISBN13: 9798992558540

Phynne~Belle, witchy-woman poet from the Bay Area, bespelling you with verse one poem at a time.

hil hoover, overgrown street rat and ringleader of The Cheese Cartel who learned how to write from discarded pulp comics. "I'll scribble you an epic for some Époisses de Bourgogne." Author of *These God-Forsaken Notes: An Irreverent Poet's Memory Loss Memoir* ISBN13: 9798986140636

About **EYEPUBLISHEWE**

Eyepublishewe is a brand new publishing company, founded in San Francisco. Art, music, video, poetry, and other literature will find inclusive shelter here. Quality work produced by the artists' hearts, minds, and souls rather than commercial interests will have this as a home. All are welcomed with open minds and hearts and eyes to the future. Together we will publish art for humanity's sake.

EPE Titles

The Green Notebook: *Poems on Family, Relationships, Spirituality, Self-Enquiry, Recovery, ACA, Disruption, Death, Walking Through the Mirror, and Cats* by **John Angell Grant** ISBN:979-8-9870259-6-3

Morning Tanka: *A journal of thank you notes between lovers, California poems in the style of traditional Japanese form poetry, translated by Yuri Miki* by **Dane Ince** and **Mercedes Dugger** ISBN: 979-8-9898764-0-2

Where Grasses Bend: *Poems from Portland to Steens Mountain in the Time of Plagues* by **Mimi German** ISBN: 979-8-9870259-5-6

Crimson Stain: *Poems Inspired by King's Letter from Jail, Real Life, and A Facet of Blood Diamond Culture* by **Dee Allen.** ISBN: 979-8-9898764-3-3

Destiny Murder!: *A Poetic Odyssey of Pulp Poems in the Beat Noir Style Concerning the Dutch Angle of Strange Dreams, Erotic, Ambivalent, Cruel and Cynical* by **Dane Ince** ISBN: 979-8-9870259-8-7

EPE Titles Coming Soon

A House without Walls: *Existential Journeys and Love Poems to Mexico* by **Lesley Constable**

La Naturaleza del Amor: *Poems in Spanish and English* by **Martin Del Toro Gutierrez**

www.ingramcontent.com/pod-product-compliance
Lightning Source LLC
Chambersburg PA
CBHW031337010826
48972CB00012B/829